Finally. A century of direct response wisdom (and test results) distilled into one easy-to-read volume! Craig and Brian have done a great service to the entire marketing community. I am sharing this with all my copy cubs TODAY!

—CLAYTON MAKEPEACE, WORLD RENOWNED COPYWRITER, EDUCATOR, AND SPEAKER

The Advertising Solution is a "short course," tour de force primer, on the very best of direct marketing principles that universally endure and profoundly perform. Brian Kurtz and Craig Simpson have produced a rather unexpected and integrative tour guide for grasping decisively how the most powerful, profitable, and predictive direct response performance principles were discovered, then take you on a no-nonsense, non-theoretical, totally actionable distillation and experimental application guide for how to apply these methods right now, in whichever market you choose, to form an activity you do—with consistently increased performance—and a bottom line that boosts results.

—JAY ABRAHAM, GLOBAL MARKETING EXPERT, SPEAKER, AND AUTHOR

Want a free, two-minute lesson in the creation of desire? Then right now, read over the table of contents of this life-changing book. See how, in less than two minutes, it creates an irresistible desire to own it. Then realize that this is exactly the knowledge you need to sell your own product or service. Whatever your field, your ability to create instant, irresistible desire will greatly leverage your success and wealth. But don't take my word for any of this. Try this two-minute table of contents challenge now and see how it's done. Then go and do likewise.

—GARY BENCIVENGA, MASTER COPYWRITER AND PUBLISHER OF MARKETING BULLETS

My quick diagnosis for how serious a copywriter or marketer is—or how much potential he or she has—is the answer to the question: "Who are your heroes?" Direct response advertising (the kind of advertising that works best on the internet) was not invented yesterday or even ten years ago. Everything—and I mean everything—that works online today is based on principles. These principles were first sorted out decades ago by giants who tested literally billions of dollars worth of ads, offers and selling strategies over the course of their careers. Put aside the latest internet "fad of the day" and read *The Advertising Solution* and get to know these giants. Make them your new best friends. It's the surest way to get rich that I know.

—KEN MCCARTHY, THESYSTEMSEMINAR.COM

Two master practitioners (not academic theorists) and experts in direct-response advertising, Craig Simpson and Brian Kurtz, have done a magnificent job profiling and extracting million-dollar lessons from past, true legends of advertising and copywriting. It will not surprise anyone who knows me: I do not agree with everything in their book, but I certainly recommend it. Those under-informed by history and legacy consistently work harder than necessary for poorer results than available. No one engaged in or spending their or their client's money on advertising should skip this master class.

—DAN S. KENNEDY, DIRECT MARKETING STRATEGIST AND COPYWRITER, AUTHOR OF THE *NO B.S.* SERIES

I personally read the works of these advertising giants while we were building Guthy|Renker and they were invaluable. I still read them today. Now Simpson and Kurtz have synthesized, selected and distilled their collective genius, originally contained within multiple volumes, into one best-of can't-put-down book, which is a must-have for any marketer. If Gary Halbert were alive today he'd promise you that this book would get you "maximum results in minimum time."

—GREG RENKER, CO-FOUNDER GUTHY|RENKER

When I started my first online business back in 1996, I quickly realized it was a direct marketing business—and that one distinction has made all the difference. But there was virtually no one teaching online marketing back them, so I went back to "old school" direct marketing to learn the craft—including the six legends featured in this book. Their work is timeless and powerful, but it can also be dense and difficult to get through. That's why it's exciting that Craig Simpson and Brian Kurtz have distilled (and updated) their wisdom into a one volume that cuts right to the heart of direct marketing.

—JEFF WALKER, AUTHOR OF THE NEW YORK TIMES' BESTSELLER LAUNCH

The Advertising Solution is a master manual which you should build into your copy, based on six masters. If you use this book as your "make sure we don't miss anything" checklist, no promotion you write will ever leave a gaping hole. I especially recommend this for the new writer who doesn't have enough street experience to be sure which sales elements are performing the heavy lifting. At the top of the list is Gary Halbert's most important technique for writing copy in Chapter 7. This is from the guy who did more to transform copywriting into a cult-following passion than anyone who came before him . . . or since.

—PERRY MARSHALL, AUTHOR OF ULTIMATE GUIDE TO GOOGLE ADWORDS, 80/20 SALES & MARKETING, AND EVOLUTION 2.0

Simply put: If you're a marketer of any sort, and consider yourself a professional—this is a must-read book. Period. After reading this book, you'll have the ability to see things other marketers cannot, spot opportunities others overlook, and avoid land mines your competitors will walk right into. History repeats itself. And the deeper your understanding of the past is the further you can see into the future.

—RYAN LEVESQUE, NATIONAL BESTSELLING AUTHOR OF ASK., CREATOR OF THE ASK METHOD™, WWW.ASKMETHOD.COM

Craig and Brian have extracted and refined pure platinum from the six greatest practitioners of people-driven marketing—Hopkins, Collier, Caples, Ogilvy, Schwartz, and Halbert—and share how their techniques and wisdom—that sold billions of dollars' worth of products and services back when a billion dollars was real money—are just as powerful in today's digital world. I wish to hell I had this treasury when I started out and could have used it as a refresher course throughout my career.

—Denny Hatch, Author and Founder of the
Who's Mailing What! Newsletter

My career has been heavily shaped by the legacy and advice of past legends (including a 20-year close friendship with Gary Halbert), and I can't recommend studying these guys enough. I've known Brian for decades, and remain in awe of his business savvy. He excelled in one of the most brutal markets in direct response, wrangling a Who's Who stable of legendary copywriters (and squeezing some of their best work out of them) . . . so he's had a front-row seat in what works, what doesn't work, and what's worth learning in this crazy modern business world. And from all I've heard, Craig has had his own incredible experiences in that same rough and tumble world of direct marketing.
Good for Brian and Craig for putting this together.

—John Carlton, Author of Simple Success Secrets No One Told You
About, www.John-Carlton.com

Since direct response advertising is the oxygen that makes your business work, understanding it is critical. Brian Kurtz and Craig Simpson have done a great job piecing together the techniques, concepts, and strategies of six of the most effective direct response advertisers who ever lived—and laid it all out for you on a gold platter in The Advertising Solution. If you want your business to have increased revenue and sales, then read this book and apply the timeless principles and strategies in it.

—Joe Polish, Founder of Genius Network and Piranha Marketing, Inc.

The six legends profiled in *The Advertising Solution* are the pioneers most of whom I studied early in my career. What I learned I truly believe was the basis of my success in direct marketing. The advice in in this book is timeless as all the principles still apply today. To have these six legends featured in one book is brilliant. Anybody will benefit from reading the lessons of just a few of the legends let alone six. I strongly recommend this book for anybody who wants to master everything from basic copywriting to the power of the internet.

—Joseph Sugarman, Author and Chairman of
BluBlocker Corporation and JS&A Group, Inc.

To see further you must stand on the shoulders of giants. Marketing and advertising is the lifeblood for any successful business and by studying these six legends profiled in *The Advertising Solution* you'll gain an unfair advantage. To me, the best ideas come from going back to the source. Twenty-first century digital marketing is all based on the fundamental strategies outlined here. The tactics will change like the blowing winds but these key principles are bedrock.

—Yanik Silver, Author of *Evolved Enterprise*

THE
ADVERTISING
SOLUTION

INFLUENCE PROSPECTS, MULTIPLY SALES, AND PROMOTE YOUR BRAND

WITH LESSONS FROM THE LEGENDS

ROBERT COLLIER

CLAUDE HOPKINS

JOHN CAPLES

DAVID OGILVY

GARY HALBERT

EUGENE SCHWARTZ

CRAIG SIMPSON with BRIAN KURTZ

EP
Entrepreneur
PRESS®

Entrepreneur Press, Publisher
Cover Design: Andrew Welyczko
Production and Composition: Eliot House Productions

This publication is designed to provide accurate and authoritative information
in regard to the subject matter covered. It is sold with the understanding that
the publisher is not engaged in rendering legal, accounting or other professional
services. If legal advice or other expert assistance is required, the services of a
competent professional person should be sought.

Library of Congress Cataloging-in-Publication Data
  Names: Simpson, Craig, 1974– author. | Kurtz, Brian, author.
  Title: The advertising solution: influence prospects, multiply sales, and
      promote your brand / by Craig Simpson with Brian Kurtz.
  Description: Irvine, California: Entrepreneur Press, 2016.
  Identifiers: LCCN 2016019781| ISBN 978-1-59918-596-5 (paperback) |
      ISBN 1-59918-596-2 (paperback)
  Subjects: LCSH: Advertising. | Advertising copy. | Marketing—Management.
      | BISAC: BUSINESS & ECONOMICS / Advertising & Promotion. |
      BUSINESS & ECONOMICS / Marketing / General. | BUSINESS &
      ECONOMICS / Business Writing.
  Classification: LCC HF5823 .S5624 2016 | DDC 659.1—dc23
  LC record available at https://lccn.loc.gov/2016019781

Printed in the United States of America

20 19 18   10 9 8 7 6 5 4 3

CONTENTS

ACKNOWLEDGMENTS

I WANT TO SAY A HUGE THANK YOU to Ellen Dickstein, my personal friend and editor. Without the countless hours she spent helping me, this book would not have been possible!

Thanks to Brian Kurtz for his friendship, wonderful insights, and guidance. Brian's interest, enthusiasm, and unique point of view made a great addition to the book.

Much appreciation goes to my family for supporting me in the penning of this book. Thank you Heidi, Aiden, Quinton, and Ziann!

It has been a pleasure to work with the team at Entrepreneur Press who provided excellent support and editorial feedback.

Last, but not least, thanks to Jeff Herman, my literary agent.

PREFACE

ALL IT AN ALLERGY: I have little or no tolerance for advertising that is not accountable—and measurable—complete with metrics that tell us whether we made money and whether we should continue. The natural next step, of course, is to then do anything we can to beat the winning promotion, again using the metrics of direct marketing.

I learned at the outset of my career to always focus on measurable response—media that pays out—and for the most part, I try to avoid getting sucked into using (or buying) advertising or marketing that relies on anyone's best guess as to whether it works.

So when Craig Simpson asked me to work with him on *The Advertising Solution*, I was inclined to say yes immediately (because it was Craig), but I wondered if I was really the right guy for the job.

After all, as I have written and often said, non-direct marketing forms of advertising—such as public relations, publicity, and even general advertising (the kind with no relationship to direct response and measurability)—usually give me hives. I used to speak at events for college students and explain that direct marketing was the only kind of marketing to practice since it's the only marketing that lets you know how you are doing all the time. I told them, "If you are needy and crave constant feedback on how you are doing, direct marketing is for you."

I also told them that making money is nice, but the real key is once we make money, we can go on to make a much bigger impact. Without focusing on measurable results, we have little or no chance to make our maximum impact.

But *The Advertising Solution*? I just wasn't sure about this one.

Then Craig explained that he was using the word "advertising" in its broadest sense to include direct marketing. And furthermore, he was going back to the original advertising geniuses who invented the methods for measuring response that are the groundwork of what we do today. As Craig said to me, "We are going to explore in depth the groundbreaking work of six legends of advertising, marketing, and copywriting and bring to life some of their most important techniques and concepts, many of them implemented almost 100 years ago. The thesis will be that what they invented is actually the foundation all marketing is based on today. If we want to work most effectively, we have to go back to the source."

So Craig didn't have me at "hello"—but he had me now. I realized at that moment that Craig and I think about the world of direct response marketing the same way, and I was all in on this project.

▪ ▪ ▪

I have talked about my life's mission to be the bridge between the truths of direct marketing of the past and how those eternal truths can be applied to everything we deem state-of-the-art in today's multichannel marketing world . . . and on into the future.

And it's amazing how well the six legends highlighted in this book realized the importance of measurability, testing, and what makes people tick (and buy) without a computer, the internet—or even Facebook.

Imagine that.

And it's astonishing to see how much they understood, clarified, and demonstrated principles that have become the lifeblood of all we do in marketing today—both offline and on. Regardless of what type of promotions you are doing today, whether it's direct advertising, online sales, blogging, self-promotion, or anything else, these are the principles you must understand—and use. They are as vital and practical today as they were when they were first put forward.

You can save years of trial and error, and increase your level of success, by putting into practice the ideas you will find in this book. I have long been a student in one way or another of these six incredible men—true heroes to myself and so many others—so the opportunity to collaborate with Craig on this book is a dream come true.

■ ■ ■

Choosing these six legends was easy given their contributions.

▌ *Claude Hopkins* wrote *Scientific Advertising*; knowing that he published his masterpiece in 1923 and that it still holds up today tells you a bit about how influential he was then ... and now. Remember, he promoted this concept in a time when there was really very little "science" available. His book is one of very few on a list I recommend to anyone beginning a marketing career today.

▌ *Robert Collier* wrote *The Robert Collier Letter Book*—a dense read—in 1937, with enough lessons in writing sales letters for a lifetime. While it is not talked about as a "must read" as often as the masterpieces from some of our other legends, Craig and I learned as much from studying how Collier dissected the sales letter as we did from anything else in this book. Collier, despite being relatively unknown (and less read), might have been the premier sales letter copywriter—ever. It is so satisfying to expose Collier's wisdom to a new generation.

▮ *John Caples* was probably the first person to understand direct marketing measurement, metrics, and testing methodology. *Tested Advertising Methods* is in its fifth edition and is still a must read for anyone who writes copy or promotes anything in any medium. The fact that this bible of proven advertising techniques has continuously been updated to reflect all the changes in marketing today tells us that Caples was clearly on to something.

▮ *David Ogilvy* was a direct marketer trapped in a general advertiser's body. He was a true creative genius and pioneer who understood direct marketing before it was ever talked about separately from advertising. He did not, as he put it:

> . . . *regard advertising as entertainment or an art form, but as a medium of information. When I write an advertisement, I don't want you to tell me that you find it "creative." I want you to find it so interesting that you buy the product.*

He did that very effectively.

▮ *Gary Halbert* is a legend whom I had the pleasure of meeting, and his influence has expanded even many years after his premature death. Over the years, I have met dozens of copywriters he mentored, some of whom are the best copywriters in the world today. I don't know of one great copywriter working today who has not studied him, learned from him, and continuously reread the incredible body of work he left behind in "swipe files" readily available to everyone. Through his writings and interviews, he continues to influence the marketplace in a major way.

▮ *Eugene Schwartz*, the one legend I knew well and someone I can call a mentor, was (and still is) as influential as anyone who has written copy or marketed products in the history of advertising. His landmark book, *Breakthrough Advertising*, is considered the most important book ever written on copy-writing, creativity, and human behavior. Schwartz was able to get into the psyche of all the audiences he wrote to—and the clients he worked intimately with—and in this book, we also share his methodology for writing efficiently and effectively. I know many copywriters today who follow Schwartz's system almost like a religion.

■ ■ ■

I think there's a theme worth noting about these six "old-timers":

The universal truths they wrote about are timeless.

Yes, some things will sound and feel outdated since they are not talking about social media or anything digital, but I encourage you to suspend your disbelief a bit as you read this book and consider how much of their work has stood the test of time. It transcends technology.

To help you, this book is filled with modern-day examples and advice on how to apply these truths to any kind of promotion you are doing today. One of my favorite quotes is from one of the great advertising men of all time, Bill Bernbach:

Adapt your techniques to an idea, not an idea to your techniques.

I don't want to get too dramatic here, but these guys are our "builders of the pyramids," creating something incredible without the use of modern technology. We are extremely proud that this book will enable the next generation of the best marketers on the planet to apply their genius in the most innovative ways. If our six legends were alive today, they would see the internet as the ultimate direct response medium. They would have a field day applying their genius to marketing online (especially because they would not have to pay for postage).

I believe one of the other great things about this book is that it makes the legends' work more accessible to today's marketers. Some of the books these men wrote can be a little difficult to get through, as they were written in a style that sounds a bit foreign to us today. We have taken the essence of each of these greats and made it easy for you to understand, assimilate, and start applying to your own work. Basically, we have created, in one volume, a way for you to take advantage of these legends' genius without having to read everything they wrote.

At least not yet.

Perhaps, once you understand the true value of Hopkins, Collier, Caples, Ogilvy, Halbert, and Schwartz, you will want more. Fortunately, much of their writing and wisdom is readily available.

▉ ▉ ▉

In general, this book will be of interest to anyone who enjoys history and would like to learn the ins and outs of how advertising works. More specifically, as a marketer, you will find it of value if you fall into one of these three groups:

1. *First-time marketers of products or services.* If you are getting into direct marketing today, it is probable that your work will mostly be online. It's also probable you will want to deliver digital content, as opposed to a physical product, if you are involved in the delivery of information.

   Despite our legends operating pre-internet, everything they talk about is applicable to today's digital marketing environment as well as the direct mail environment. You will see that throughout this book as we make specific mention of online and offline applications of our legends' knowledge.

   Through my 35-plus years in direct marketing, as we went from horse and buggy (i.e., direct mail/print only) to the automobile (online), the smartest marketers I knew always diversified their distribution channels just as they would diversify their investment portfolio. Hopefully you believe as I do that "multichannel marketing" should always be at the top of one's mind.

   What these legends were able to accomplish in print and direct mail is astounding, and everything they did is applicable to how we launch new products and sell our services today. And note: offline media still scales quite well and often delivers more engaged customers with higher lifetime value. So we encourage you to consider offline techniques to complement your online business when appropriate. Our legends will help you with both.

2. *Experienced marketers who have never heard of these six legends.* If you are successfully marketing goods and services today, and you are focused mostly (or even exclusively) online, why would you want or need to read about advertising greats of the past who did everything offline? This question is understandable, and it is one of the motivations Craig and I had for writing this book.

   While you may not have heard of any (or all) of the men we profile here, I believe you can take almost anything in this book and apply it to your current online marketing plan. And if you are marketing offline, you really need to know about these six legends so you can produce your best work.

   Another motivation for us to write this book was to make sure that Hopkins, Collier, Caples, Ogilvy, Halbert, and Schwartz are never forgotten. If we can introduce them to an audience of world-class marketers who aren't aware of them yet, we will know we have done something special. Their contributions to advertising, direct response marketing, and creative development are as deep as they are wide.

   Some information in this book may simply serve as reminders for experienced marketers, but hopefully all the material will lead to inspiration and new breakthroughs in how you sell and promote.

   As a popular saying tells us:

   > *Learn the rules like a pro, so you can break them like an artist.*

3. *Experienced marketers who are actually old enough to remember these six legends.* If you fall in this category, I'm guessing you know many of these principles, and you may have learned them first from one of the legends we profile in this book.

But are there basics you have forgotten? Is it time for some reminders of what got you here?

For this group, I believe reading this book will be much more than a stroll down memory lane. I think it will offer one reinforcement and one inspiration after another so you too can continue to "break the rules like an artist."

▊ ▊ ▊

Finally, on the surface, I may look like a direct-marketing hypocrite—that is, I claim to have been a slave to measurable and accountable advertising my whole life, yet I've got my name attached to a book about six men who are eternally tied in people's minds to a world of general advertising that was often more about brand and image than about getting orders and making money.

But after poring over the work of these legends, it is clear to me that whenever they could, they bucked the trend of clients paying them to do pretty ads that made someone in a boardroom feel great about their brand, product, or image. Instead, they strove to prove the worth of the work they produced. This is why I think this book is so important—despite the possibility that some may come to it under the misapprehension that it's about "general advertising."

You will see throughout the pages of this book that our legends were way ahead of their time. They invented today's methods for determining whether marketing is providing the desired return on investment.

The life's work of our legends needed to be shared in a volume like this, and I thank Craig for asking me to be part of it. I sincerely hope you will gain as much by applying the eternal truths covered in this book as the two of us do every day, working with marketers in every category and in every medium. Therefore, I am the proudest direct-marketing hypocrite who ever lived. I'll wear that title like a badge of honor—I hope you will too.

—Brian Kurtz, Titans Marketing LLC

INTRODUCTION

*T*HE ADVERTISING SOLUTION: *Influence Prospects, Multiply Sales, and Promote Your Brand* distills the wisdom of the world's greatest promotional pioneers, expressing their basic principles in the language of today, so that you can have the information you need to become a master marketer. In addition, by understanding these principles, you can become a more astute judge of the advertising you're exposed to every day.

Products and business models change over time, but human nature does not. The same principles of human desire and methods of influence that guided the markets of ancient Greece are still operating today. In order to get people to do what you want them to do, you have to understand what motivates them. You also have to know how to present yourself and your product to get their interest, their trust, and ultimately their willingness to call you, visit you, or send you their money.

For most of human history, communication between the seller and the buyer was one-on-one. That changed with the development of printing and the expansion of literacy. Sellers could print fliers and tracts. They could place ads in newssheets. Popular pictorial magazines, largely supported with ad revenue, began to be published.

With the development of the large mail order companies, such as Montgomery Ward and Sears, Roebuck and Co., came the growth of another form of advertising—direct mail. Then, starting in the 20th century, radio and television allowed sellers to reach a huge captive audience. And of course today we have the internet, allowing marketers, bloggers, and promoters of all types to reach untold numbers of individuals at all hours of the day and night.

During the early part of the 20th century—as new ways to reach large numbers of people became available—a new breed of salesperson came into existence. Before that, writing advertising copy was a side job. But it soon became apparent that writing effective ads required a special kind of skill and dedicated effort. You couldn't rely on your secretary to write ad copy during spare moments. If you wanted to grow your business, you needed a talented individual who understood human nature and was willing to scientifically test ads to find out what worked and what didn't.

Thus dawned a golden age of advertising, driven by legendary marketers like Robert Collier, Claude Hopkins, John Caples, David Ogilvy, Eugene Schwartz, and Gary Halbert. These ad men knew what motivated people, they knew how to write copy that kept prospects reading and moved them to take action, and they knew how to experiment and test what they produced so they could keep honing their message to get the best results.

Anyone today who wishes to influence people would benefit greatly from learning the basic principles discovered by these advertising legends. But few do, either because they haven't heard of these promotional giants, or because they find the older men's way of expressing themselves dated and hard to understand.

That's a shame, because what these legendary ad men have to share about the principles of effective advertising is just as fresh and relevant today as it was back when they first shared their findings with others. Anyone who is in the business of influencing other people would become much more successful by understanding what these men discovered long ago.

Whether you're a business owner writing your own ad copy, a professional copywriter working for clients, a web developer writing homepage copy for e-tail sites, someone placing listings on eBay or craigslist, or a blogger who is essentially writing copy to sell yourself, you would do a much better job of accomplishing your goals if you understood the universal principles of human nature and advertising presented here in *The Advertising Solution*.

—Craig Simpson, Simpson Direct, Inc.

CHAPTER 1

MEET THE LEGENDS WHO CREATED THE RULES OF MODERN PROMOTIONS

THERE HAVE BEEN MANY GREAT promoters and copywriters over the years, and we salute them all. But in this book, we're going to focus on the real legends—the great marketing and advertising minds from the past who practically created the industry as we know it, and who continue to have a tremendous influence today.

Their discoveries and insights into what it takes to move others to action are as fresh and alive and relevant today as they were when they were first used to create powerhouse, record-breaking publicity and sales materials. These were colorful, creative individuals who invented the rules for promoting their products and themselves. And their rules work as well now as they did then. In this book, we will delve into their discoveries and how we can use them today. First, let's learn a little about the lives of each of these remarkable individuals.

CLAUDE HOPKINS: THE FIRST SCIENTIST OF ADVERTISING

Claude C. Hopkins (1866–1932) was an advertising pioneer from the first part of the 20th century. His highly influential 1923 book *Scientific Advertising* introduced the world of advertising to principles like test marketing, the use of coupons and free samples, key coding ads to make sure responses could be tracked, and thoroughly researching a product to create meaningful copy instead of fluff.

These are all such standard practices today that we take them for granted, but they were all invented by Hopkins.

Hopkins believed that advertising had just one purpose: to sell something. That meant that advertising was to be judged by one measure only: the sales that were the direct result of the ad.

For each of his ads, Hopkins measured the cost per customer and the cost per sale. These were the yardsticks by which he compared his results so he could fine-tune his ads with each campaign. Then he turned his findings into principles that he applied and tested in campaigns for other products.

His campaigns were wildly successful, largely due to his thoroughly researched "reason why" copy. As a result, in 1907 he was hired by the Lord & Thomas advertising agency for the then unheard-of salary of $185,000 a year. (At the time, a professor at Harvard made less than $1,000 per year.)

In his autobiography, *My Life in Advertising*, Hopkins attributed much of his success to his Scotch mother, who "typified in a high degree the thrift and caution, the intelligence, ambition, and energy of her race." From her he inherited "conspicuous conservatism," and believed it was the lack of this quality that wrecked more advertisers and businesspeople than anything else. Hopkins called "safety first" his guiding star, which meant he took no chances in spending his clients' money or creating campaigns on which the success of their businesses rested. The result was scientific advertising.

He also attributed much of his success to his father, a newspaperman who was the son of a poor clergyman. Hopkins grew up in poverty, which gave him an understanding of the poor and working class: what they wanted, what their struggles were. These were to become his future customers, and he knew how to talk to them so that they would see him as one of their own. If you are promoting anything, you must understand your audience—and make them know that you understand them—if you hope to influence them.

From an early age he made money by selling items door to door. He worked hard to support his family after his father died when Hopkins was only ten, which taught him a great deal about how to get his foot in the door. Once he did, he almost always made a sale. This experience, and his natural creativity, enabled him to see the broader picture when it came to selling. It was also during this time that he learned the value of giving free samples and coupons, which became the cornerstone of many of his later campaigns.

Hopkins originally planned to become a clergyman, but his philosophies didn't suit the strict church structure of the time. So he looked for another way to earn his living.

He didn't enter advertising right away, but started off as a bookkeeper for the Bissell carpet sweeper company in Grand Rapids, Michigan. He soon saw an opportunity in helping them write sales copy, although his bosses disagreed with his ideas. They wanted to sell the mechanics of the sweeper. But he believed that to appeal to female buyers, they should stress the design and beauty of the different kinds of wood he had advised the company to use in the sweepers. Although they dragged their feet, company executives ultimately went along with his ideas because they brought results— and you couldn't argue with the results. One pamphlet Hopkins designed, promoting a special limited edition sweeper made from an exotic wood, sold more sweepers in six weeks than the company had managed in a full year.

From there, he became a full-time ad man, writing copy for products like lard, chicken incubators, shoes, medical products, liquefied ozone—the list goes on. Finally, as an executive and ultimately president of the Lord & Thomas advertising agency, his campaigns for big-name products like Palmolive, Quaker Oats, and Pepsodent Toothpaste really put him on the map.

The success of his campaigns largely rested on what he called "traced advertising." Hopkins had no respect for unproven theories of advertising. He said each ad is a salesman, and you had to compare their response rates, just as you would compare the success rates of salesmen in your employ, holding them responsible for their cost and results.

He acknowledged there were basic laws of advertising that were generally accepted and backed by results, and that they should be learned. However, using these basic laws didn't remove the need for scientific advertising. Every sales piece or ad, even if based on these principles, still had to be tested. We'll look at many of these principles throughout this book.

Every aspect of Hopkins' life contributed to his homespun style, his understanding of his audience, and his need to prove the effectiveness of what he created in terms of sales figures. We have much to learn from him today. The great David Ogilvy (one of the other legends profiled in this book) said:

> *Nobody should be allowed to have anything to do with advertising until he has read this book [Scientific Advertising] seven times. It changed the course of my life.*

Claude Hopkins changed not just the world of advertising and promotions, but the way we perceive the world.

ROBERT COLLIER: THE PHILOSOPHER AD MAN

Robert Collier (1885–1950) was a fabulously successful direct mail marketer who ruled the field during the first half of the 20th century. He is believed to have written sales letters that brought in upwards of $100 million during the 1920s and 1930s. Today, that would amount to $1 billion.

How did he do it? Just by writing sales letters for a wide variety of products—letters that were sent out across America and brought back tons of orders. He sold sets of *Harvard Classics*, face cream, tractors, pipes, winter coats—there was nothing he couldn't sell.

His discoveries and insight into human nature, and how he used them to manipulate interest in his products, are of tremendous practical use to promoters of all kinds today. It is well worth the effort to learn what he had to tell us in his classic works so we can increase the effectiveness of our attempts to influence others.

But Collier was more than a writer of ad copy. He was also the author of self-help books and New Thought metaphysical works, one of which, *The Secret of the Ages*, sold more than 300,000 copies during his lifetime. No doubt his understanding of people's hopes and dreams enabled him to appeal to them in a way that got them to take the action he wanted.

Collier's approach to life, which stressed abundance, visualization, faith, and confidence, recently found new fame as one of the building blocks of Rhonda Byrne's bestselling 2006 book *The Secret* and the popular movement that sprang up around it.

There are some interesting parallels between Collier's life and that of Claude Hopkins.

They both had early experience in publishing: Hopkins through his newsman father, Collier through his uncle Peter Fenelon Collier, who was the founder and publisher of the popular magazine *Collier's Weekly*. They both lost parents early in life (Hopkins lost his father, Collier lost his mother). They both had early aspirations to enter the clergy. They both turned out to be unsuited for that kind of life and headed out to make their fortune elsewhere.

Like Hopkins, Collier started out working in a manufacturing setting. He worked in the West Virginia coal industry, where he educated himself in business and writing. Spending time with local people and watching their struggles gave him another kind of education in human nature.

It was here that he wrote his first sales letter. At the time he had no experience in sales, but he was enthusiastic and had an idea for an approach that would appeal to his audience; the result was a huge success. He applied what he learned from that letter to other letters for the company, and in this way he learned his craft through trial and error.

He was also helped by some of the works on advertising that were already classics at the time. He particularly credited Herbert Watson's *Business Correspondence Library* for giving him the tools he needed.

Like Hopkins, Collier always judged his own work by the number of sales. Over time, as he experimented with different methods and weighed the results, he developed his own set of rules.

After eight years Collier moved to New York to work at his uncle's publishing business. Thanks to his years writing copy in the coal industry, he was well-prepared to start working in the advertising department, where his career really began to take off.

The rules he developed for himself to sell coal to utility companies were universal rules that also worked to sell a "five-foot shelf" of *Harvard Classics* to up-and-coming families, which was a notable direct marketing offer of its day.

Collier used testimonials, order cards, return policies, and payment plans to sell untold numbers of books. These are all techniques we take for granted today, but they were breakthroughs back then. And of course, there was the brilliance of the copy, which appealed to people's self-images and their aspirations for a better life. That's what really got their attention so that they devoured his sales letters and were then motivated to place their orders.

Collier followed up his success selling *Harvard Classics* with a campaign that sold $2 million worth of O. Henry stories. An important aspect of his success was introducing a sense of *urgency*. People had to order by a certain date to receive a bonus item with their purchase. This technique is used everywhere today.

In his advertising primer, *The Robert Collier Letter Book*, Collier analyzed the letters from many of his major campaigns. As we learn why he tried certain techniques and see how they turned out, we become aware of how much thoughtful insight Collier applied to each of his sales letters. He didn't just write off the top of his head: he tried to understand the desires of his audience and then did his best to appeal to those desires and inspire his prospects to take action.

Collier taught us all a great deal about human nature. Later in this book we'll take a deep dive into learning the nuts and bolts of how he did what he did—and did as well as anyone in the history of advertising. Anyone can become more adept at influencing others by understanding how Collier did it.

JOHN CAPLES: THE MAESTRO OF HEADLINES

John Caples (1900–1990) was a dominating force in the world of direct-response advertising for most of the 20th century. His legendary career had its big start in 1926, when he wrote the fabulously successful (and often imitated) headline:

> They Laughed When I Sat Down at the Piano
> But When I Started to Play!

The ad was successful because of the *measurable response* it produced, and measuring response was what John Caples was all about. He was a proponent of measurement in advertising to prove, scientifically, whether an advertisement worked.

In today's fast-paced marketing environment, measuring results based on the specifics of your ads and where you're advertising will make or break your business. John Caples understood that a long time ago. And thank goodness we can follow his advice today. There are people advertising on Facebook or on Google AdWords who are tracking their response rates exactly as Caples suggested. Unfortunately, there are still many online marketers who just throw ads out there and don't track their results. They are missing the key point of and the opportunity in measurable response advertising. We must give Caples the credit for developing the idea of measuring response because those who follow his lead are the most successful internet marketers today.

But let's start at the beginning.

The young Caples was painfully shy, dropping out of Columbia University to avoid making a two-minute speech in front of a required English class for freshmen. Perhaps this was the basis of his famous "They Laughed" headline. He understood what it was to feel inadequate and to have a driving need to prove yourself to others—and even more, to rub your success in a naysayer's face.

Caples was a Manhattan native with successful, cultured parents. After his failure at Columbia, he was compelled to make good. So he joined the Navy with the goal of studying and preparing himself to win a position at the United States Naval Academy in Annapolis. He passed the competitive exam and graduated from the academy in 1924.

However, the Navy was downsizing after World War I, so he accepted their offer to give up his commission as an ensign. Instead he went on to earn a B.S. in engineering. A subsequent job as an engineer with the New York Telephone Company bored him to tears, and he ended up looking for vocational guidance. The counselor's report mainly pointed out all the negative factors about possible future employment situations, but he did make one recommendation: "I would not discourage you in your ambition to develop yourself as a writer."

That turned out to be golden advice.

Caples took some writing courses and decided to try a career in advertising, starting with a position at a leading mail order company, Ruthrauff & Ryan. He soon realized that the advantage of mail order advertising, as opposed to magazine ads, was that you had unarguable feedback about the success of an ad because you knew exactly how many people responded to it. That made it possible to experiment with different copy or formats to see which worked best. Those findings could then be applied to new ads, leading to more and more effective campaigns.

One of Caples' earliest campaigns was the one that made his fortune. It was a sales letter for a home-study music course with the soon-to-be-famous "They Laughed" headline, followed by four pages of copy. This headline so struck the imagination of people at the time that it took on a life of its own. Comedians even based vaudeville routines on it: "They laughed when I sat down at the piano. Someone had stolen the stool."

The "They Laughed" approach was copied by others, but no one did it as well as Caples himself, who wrote a similar ad for a correspondence French language course: "They grinned when the waiter spoke to me in French—but their laughter changed to amazement at my reply."

As Caples grew in stature as an advertiser, he moved up in the industry, eventually landing a position at BBDO, one of the largest advertising agencies of that era. He stayed there for the rest of his career, ultimately becoming vice president and creative director. What made Caples one of our legends is not only that he wrote amazingly effective copy but that he was also a scientist in his field. Undoubtedly his training as an engineer gave him the tools to become a master of testing. He explained his techniques in his classic book *Tested Advertising Methods*, which is still studied by copywriters today.

Caples developed many of the methods that define the field of advertising, such as split-run testing. With this technique, advertisers create two different ads, maybe with different headlines or layouts. They have a magazine publisher print half the run with one ad and the other half with the other ad. The ads must have some kind of reply requested so the responses to the two ads can be compared. Caples started with simple two-way split-run tests and worked up to 40-way tests. He also advocated the importance of a great headline that appealed to readers' self-interest, as well as other qualities, such as curiosity and newsworthiness. We'll be looking at these ideas and many others from Caples' groundbreaking work later in this book.

Caples combined the science of persuasion with the science of precision like no one who came before him . . . and he paved the way for all who came after.

DAVID OGILVY: THE ADVERTISING WIZARD

David Ogilvy (1911–1999) is perhaps one of the best-known of the legends we're profiling in this book. He was often referred to as "The Father of Advertising." By 1962, he'd revolutionized the way copywriters created ads, and that year *Time* magazine dubbed him "the most sought-after wizard in today's advertising industry."

Ogilvy wrote about his approach to advertising in *Confessions of an Advertising Man*, first published in 1963. Some people believe he served as the model for *Mad Men's* Don Draper. Indeed, if you look at pictures of Ogilvy, he was just as dashing as the TV character.

Ogilvy's beginnings, as with so many of the other great ad men we're looking at here, would not have suggested that he would become an "advertising man" or that he would achieve the level of success he enjoyed. Ogilvy was born in England, the son of an Anglo-Irish mother and a Gaelic-speaking Scotsman. His father was a classics scholar and a financial broker—an odd combination that may explain Ogilvy's own wide-ranging interests.

The family did not have much money, but Ogilvy's talents allowed him to win scholarships, including one to Oxford. He didn't relish the academic life, however, and dropped out of Oxford before he could graduate. Then he moved to Paris, where he became a kitchen worker at the Hotel Majestic. The work there was exhausting, so he soon ended up back in Great Britain, where he sold cooking stoves door to door for the AGA Rangemaster Company. His success was so marked that the company asked him to write up a manual for their other salesmen. According to *Fortune* magazine, it was "probably the best sales manual ever written."

One of Ogilvy's principal rules for selling stoves is one we often hear in some form or other today:

The more prospects you talk to, the more sales you expose yourself to, the more orders you will get.

Even at a very young age, Ogilvy understood that selling is a numbers game.

Restless to expand his horizons, Ogilvy moved to the United States in 1938 and took a position with George Gallup's Audience Research Institute in New Jersey. It was here that he learned the value of following rigorous research methodology, which served him well later as he developed lucrative ad campaigns for his clients.

When World War II broke out, he joined the Intelligence Service, housed in the British Embassy in Washington, DC. He realized the potential in applying the techniques he had learned at Gallup to the field of secret intelligence and wrote a report outlining his ideas. General Eisenhower got wind of the report and implemented its suggestions during the final year of the war, with great success. Ogilvy was involved in other propaganda activities during the war that laid a strong foundation for his later career in advertising.

After the war Ogilvy bought a farm in Lancaster County, Pennsylvania, which he valued for its serenity. However, he soon realized he wasn't cut out to be a farmer and moved to New York to begin the next chapter of his life. With only a smattering of advertising experience, he founded the ad agency Hewitt, Ogilvy, Benson & Mather, which eventually joined with the London agency Mather & Crowther to become Ogilvy & Mather Worldwide. Finally, our Renaissance man had really come into his own as an advertiser.

His client list boasted an impressive array of brand names in many diverse industries: Rolls-Royce, Shell, Lever Brothers, General Foods, Sears, Hathaway Shirts, Schweppes, and American Express. He and his team created such successful campaigns that new clients begged to be taken on. As Ogilvy put it:

> *I doubt whether any copywriter has ever had so many winners in such a short period of time. They made Ogilvy & Mather so hot that getting clients was like shooting fish in a barrel.*

Several factors went into making Ogilvy the premier advertiser of his time. First, he was a brilliant writer as well as a brilliant observer. He knew how to recognize a genius idea when he saw it. Second, he had respect for his target audience. He loathed the kind of advertising that talked down to people. He believed the way to sell to people was to talk to them as though they were intelligent. He was famous for telling other ad writers:

The customer is not a moron, she's your wife.

Ogilvy's methods were also a big factor in his success. We'll be looking at these in greater detail throughout this book, but like so many of the other legends we're profiling, he didn't just make things up because they sounded good. He immersed himself in information about a product and let his ads almost write themselves.

Beyond his genius for recognizing the "big idea," Ogilvy lived by the principles of respecting your audience and basing pitches on the actual qualities of whatever it is you are trying to sell, whether it's a product or a person. Both are critical for anyone in the business of promotion.

EUGENE SCHWARTZ: THE BREAKTHROUGH ADVERTISER

Eugene Schwartz (1927–1995) was a master copywriter during the mid- to late-20th century. He was said to have known what "makes people tick," and this understanding led him to be one of the most successful copywriters of all time. What separated Schwartz from other ad writers, then and now, is that he knew that what underlies human behavior is the key to writing breakthrough copy.

Schwartz specialized in writing for direct mail campaigns, and his sales pieces sold hundreds of millions of dollars' worth of product for his fortunate clients. He was the genius who helped turn a small-business newsletter into the huge mega-publisher Boardroom Inc. (now Bottom Line Inc.), which became one of the most successful publishing companies of its kind.

He was also responsible for some of the most successful direct-mail campaigns ever run by Rodale Inc., known for iconic brands like *Prevention* magazine and health books that changed millions of lives. It's said they once paid him $54,000 for four hours of work—and it was well worth it!

Oddly enough, although Schwartz was one of the greatest copywriters of his day, these days he is one of the most elusive. Some current writers speak of him with reverence, touting him as the greatest ad man who ever lived. But the book where he revealed so many of his secrets, *Breakthrough Advertising*, published in 1966, is out of print; only rare copies are available from Amazon and other sources for hundreds of dollars.

It's impressive that Schwartz's book was written back in 1966, and yet not one word has been changed in the current limited edition (originally reissued by Bottom Line Books, a division of Bottom Line Inc., and now in the hands of my friend and collaborator Brian Kurtz at Titans Marketing LLC). *Breakthrough Advertising* has become a cult classic. People are constantly asking Brian for copies of the book, and many copywriters today consider it their bible. The book is still 100 percent relevant for advertisers today because it is as much about essential human behavior as it is about writing breakthrough copy.

Here's another interesting fact about Schwartz: when his obituary appeared in *The New York Times*, the headline read "Eugene Schwartz, 68, Modern-Art Collector, Dies." The first line read, "Eugene M. Schwartz, who with his wife, Barbara, assembled one of the nation's leading collections of contemporary art, died yesterday at his home in Manhattan." Lest you think they were talking about some other Eugene Schwartz, the obituary added, almost as an afterthought:

> *An advertising copywriter whose specialty was direct mail campaigns, Mr. Schwartz was the author of ten books, including* Breakthrough Advertising *and* The Brilliance Breakthrough. *He wrote some of the most celebrated lines in direct mail advertising, such as 'Give Me 15 Minutes and I'll Give You a Super-Power Memory,' which launched the first book of the memory expert Harry Lorraine. But it was as an enthusiastic lover of art that Mr. Schwartz was best known.*

The remainder of the article then went on to talk only of his art collections and donations.

If you search for Eugene Schwartz on the internet, you arrive at a number of questionable websites that say you can download his classic book for free, but the process is a little scary and smacks of being a scam. Other sites offer "swipe files" of his most famous ads, or courses on how to write like Eugene Schwartz. You can also find some books written about Schwartz, and transcripts of talks he gave that are so charming and revealing it makes one long to get one's hands on his book. A lot of the information on Schwartz's work that you will read here is based on those transcripts.

Another invaluable resource has been Brian's experience working directly with Schwartz on his promotions for Boardroom Inc. and his consultation with Schwartz about Schwartz's own publishing business, Instant Improvement. Brian's familiarity gives us much insight into this icon of copywriting and a bit of the "inside scoop."

Like many of our other legends, Schwartz did not come from a big city, nor did he have a sophisticated background. He was born in Butte, Montana, and later claimed that his upbringing in Middle America gave him an understanding of the interests and values of the people he would later be writing for.

When he moved to New York City in his early 20s, he joined the advertising firm of Huber Hoge & Sons as a messenger boy. Through hard work and talent, he climbed the ladder to copy chief. Five years later, at just 27, he went out on his own and perfected the unique methods and approach to promotion we'll be studying here.

It's interesting to look at something Schwartz wrote about his art collecting, which he pursued out of a love of art, not for its value as an investment:

The only important thing about art is the art itself—not its monetary value, not its social prestige, not its public-relations leverage.

I think this says a lot about his approach to writing sales letters. His interest was in the product itself, what it was, and what it could do. He didn't try to appeal to people's desire for prestige, and he didn't try to impress them with his writing style or intellect.

Schwartz could have written to the most sophisticated and intelligent audiences if he chose, but he preferred to write about products and topics that excited him. It didn't matter if the subject was considered "less sophisticated." He was well-read in many disciplines and could write on almost any subject without talking down to prospects. He always wrote on their terms, with the highest integrity.

He let the product—and how it could help the reader—speak for itself. Everything was upfront and honest. This again is a great tip to keep in mind for all of us, whatever we might be trying to promote.

As a side note to indicate Schwartz's forward thinking: Some of the copy he wrote for Rodale and Boardroom was not for money but in exchange for rights to their huge mailing lists of people interested in health. He would then mail sales pieces to these lists for his own small publishing company, Instant Improvement. Schwartz knew that getting paid for copy was one way to go, but better yet was to get names to build his own business. He understood that the combination of the right copy with a great list, targeted to the product, was the key to success. This is a great lesson for marketers of today . . . and for copywriters too.

GARY HALBERT: THE GODFATHER OF COPYWRITING

Gary Halbert (1938–2007) was one of the most successful copywriters of his time, which wasn't so long ago. He died in 2007, leaving behind a legacy of super successful ad copy that sold billions of dollars' worth of product and that still serves as a kind of "textbook of higher education" for copywriters today.

Halbert wasn't just a brilliant copywriter; he was also a mentor and a tremendous inspiration to aspiring copywriters from the mid-1980s until his death. He mentored many of the best copywriters working in the industry today. He had a reputation for being very tough on his "copy cubs," but they all say his direct teaching style is what made them world-class.

Although Halbert wrote primarily for direct mail, the principles he taught cut across all media. Most of his students today are copywriters working online—some of the best out there.

His regularly published column, "The Gary Halbert Letter," revealed his secrets of great copywriting, and was eagerly pored over by newcomers and seasoned professionals alike. Halbert's style was a bit flamboyant and sometimes salty, but he understood how to get through to people's hearts and move them to action. And that was important because, as Halbert said:

Any business can be changed by a great sales letter.

Halbert was a larger-than-life character. John Carlton, world-class copywriter and an early "graduate from Halbert University," was a friend and colleague who worked with Halbert for more than 20 years, which he called "the wildest of my career." Carlton said of Halbert:

He was bigger than life and could suck the air out of any room he entered without saying a word . . . preceded only by the shock wave of his hard-earned reputation. He had a lust for experience, an astonishingly huge appetite for everything available in life, and took great pleasure in being who he was.

And he truly was a great man. He single-handedly changed the nature of modern direct response advertising . . . and through his teachings, spawned three generations (and still counting) of rabble-rousing entrepreneurs and marketers who continue to force the business world to bend to their will.

I think that says more about Halbert in four sentences than I could have said in five pages. Carlton also said that while he learned a lot from Halbert about copywriting, the lesson that most affected his life was about living well. When he first met Halbert, Carlton was an up-and-comer in the world of corporate copywriting, but was bored to tears. He worked with Halbert on some projects, until one day Halbert asked him to become his main full-time writer. That would mean giving up a sure thing—a million-dollar career—to do something that "offered a chance to be true to my own mojo."

It would be fun, with each new gig giving him the chance to work with different entrepreneurs. "I realized how little I was motivated by money," Carlton said, "and how alive I felt in the entrepreneurial world, where rules were constantly broken and reinvented, and we could field-test our wildest ideas (the ideas that made the corporate beasts squirm)."

As it turned out, Carlton made his fortune after all. The riskier path turned out to be the best one. "Gary was the first living example I'd ever met of someone who went for the gusto," he said. "And after 30 years of sharing what I've learned, I'm still not done tapping into the deep well of tactics, insight, and savvy gathered from the raw wonder of working with the man."

Halbert was often called the godfather of copywriting, possibly because he spent ten months in the Boron Federal Prison Camp (popularly known as Club Fed) in the 1980s on charges of fraud. Some people jumped to his defense and said he had been wrongly accused, but he admitted he had gone over the line and accepted his sentence. Undaunted, he called his incarceration a "vacation" and made good use of his time.

While he was in prison, he laid the groundwork for his re-emergence as a major player in the field of writing for direct marketing. He wrote a series of messages to inspire his children called *The Boron Letters*, which he said were the "most heartfelt messages that I've ever written." They were filled with his wisdom on the secrets of persuasion. These letters from prison became a cult classic among marketers and have guided untold numbers of aspiring ad writers.

Halbert was given other nicknames by his many admirers, including the "Prince of Print" and the "King of Copy." These titles showed the degree to which people both appreciated what he taught them and had genuine affection for him.

Perhaps the product Halbert sold the best was himself, and he did it just by *being* himself. He gave away his copywriting secrets for free on his website, and by doing that, he attracted clients he might never have landed in any other way. Like the other legends we're studying here, Halbert did not hold with dreaming up imaginary selling points. He also thought it was a mistake to try to impress your audience with stylish writing.

When it came to producing effective copy, Halbert recommended going to the source—your best customers—to learn exactly what they were looking for and what they found appealing in your product. Once you knew what that was, the sales piece would practically write itself.

He also understood, as many of our legends did, that you have to write to a sixth-grade level (give or take a few grades). This doesn't mean you talk down to people, but you must write in a way that attracts in as many people as possible.

Halbert perfected a writing style that was able to reach a wide number of people without ever putting them off by sounding superior. Today's writers could take a lesson from the great Gary Halbert, who knew it was crazy to write too many levels above your reader. He truly was an "everyman" writer. The fact that his disciples are able to write exquisite copy on the internet today shows that his style was universal.

One of Halbert's most successful pieces was his "Coat of Arms" direct mail letter. If you're of a certain age, you probably received one at one time or another. The letter, first sent in 1971, offered people a history of their family along with its "coat of arms." We all want to see ourselves as special, and suddenly discovering that you come from a family with a rich tradition could be a boost to the ego. Halbert certainly knew how to play to that desire.

Among the techniques Halbert either invented or developed were identifying a unique selling proposition (USP), tracking the results of your ad campaigns, using interesting formatting methods to attract and keep attention, making the most of the P.S. at the end of a letter, and employing specialized language. All these methods are the basis of much of the sales writing you find today, offline and online.

As you read this book and learn about Halbert's ideas and methods, you'll find they are of great value for any kind of promotional activity you may be engaging in today.

COMMON THREADS

We'll be going deeply into the wisdom and inspiration available in the works of all the legends we're highlighting here. But before we go on, I just want to point out some of the common threads we'll see again and again:

1. *Each of these advertising legends went way beyond simply the opinions of the day.* They all developed methods based on the truth of the product and the experience of the prospect.

2. *The prospect (i.e., the list) is paramount.* They all made an effort to understand their audience and were aided in this by their own simple beginnings that did not hint at the legendary status they'd one day achieve. They knew their list of prospects was of primary importance, and they learned all they could about them.

3. *They never talked down to people.* You may be the most brilliant person in your field, but don't show off how smart you are. Use what you know to talk to people in a way that helps them understand what you are saying. Spend some time reading our legends' works. Get a feel for how these brilliant copywriters were able to temper their writing so it appealed to the everyman.

4. *Product research is king.* Even though they were brilliant writers, they didn't turn to their imaginations to come up with sales pitches. They immersed themselves in their product, learned all they could about it, and allowed the product to tell them how to sell it.

5. *They never rested on their laurels.* They were always working to improve on every success and were willing to experiment to learn how to get greater results. As soon as they had a winner, they set out to beat their own promotion.

These are valuable points for all of us, regardless of what we might be selling. They comprise universal wisdom for the promoter of today. It's time for us to explore all the treasures in the minds of Hopkins, Collier, Caples, Ogilvy, Schwartz, and Halbert. You are about to learn the eternal truths of marketing . . . and if you think they're old news, please read on as we dispel that myth.

CHAPTER 2

CREATIVE SALESMANSHIP—A LITTLE GENIUS AND A LOT OF SWEAT

N O MATTER WHAT MEDIUM you're using to promote, it all begins with a brilliant idea—an idea that will get across to others what makes you different and special. This isn't new. This is the same challenge that has faced sellers and promoters since the ancient Babylonians sold rugs and brass cooking pots in their open markets.

Fortunately, you don't have to research the ancient Babylonians to find out how to succeed. You have the guidance of these advertising legends. They clearly laid out a set of basic principles that allow even novice promoters to take advantage of basic human psychology to attract interest and motivate behavior. In this chapter, we'll focus on the work of three of our legends: Robert Collier, David Ogilvy, and Eugene Schwartz.

TRICKS OF SHOWMANSHIP

Most of our legends worked in the hot medium of their day—direct mail. The tricks of showmanship they used helped make their letters stand out among the rest of the mail in the mailbox. What they had to say is of major importance to all marketers today—even internet marketers. It is still necessary to make an email stand out in an inbox or an online ad stand out on a webpage. Even more significantly, there are enormous possibilities in multichannel marketing, where even marketers who are exclusively online can find great profitability in adding a direct mail element to a full campaign. So keep this in mind as we delve into our subject.

We'll start with Robert Collier, whose sales letters sold millions of dollars' worth of goods back in the early part of the past century. He developed formulas and rules that he knew worked because of their measurable wide appeal to prospects who received his sales pieces and went on to order whatever he was selling. People responded positively to his images and the way he couched his arguments.

Following proven rules and a great use of language are both important to the success of a direct mail campaign. They're also essential to the success of any promotional effort, whether it involves writing a job application, creating a Facebook Page, putting together an ecommerce site—even writing a description of yourself on a dating website!

But Collier knew there was an additional element to creating effective sales letters (or any other promotional material) that was also critical to achieving positive results. It was something he called "showmanship," and he devoted a whole chapter to it in his classic work, *The Robert Collier Letter Book*. Collier opened the chapter with two examples of self-promotions, both of them created and carried out by young men who used unusual methods to get the attention of potential employers so they could land a job.

One of these young men used a variation on what we call "lumpy mail" today. He mailed a clever note in a bottle to 81 advertising agencies in which he talked about being stranded and in need of a job. The heads of personnel departments took notice, and he soon got the job he wanted. Another young man achieved success by printing his message on books of matches that he left wherever he visited. As Collier put it:

Showmanship always does get a hearing.

We're going to look at some of Collier's other great ideas on showmanship below. Of course, as noted above, most of them relate to making direct mail pieces stand out because that was his primary medium, but it's the principle of showmanship that I want you to learn. I hope Collier's examples will stimulate your creativity so you will incorporate showmanship into your own campaigns, whatever medium you use.

The Crisp Dollar Bill . . . and More!

Collier said the most successful bit of showmanship in an advertising campaign that he ever saw involved the "Dollar Bill" letter. Pinned to the top of the letter was a real dollar bill. If you received a letter with a dollar bill attached to it today, that would get your attention. Imagine how much attention it got back in the 1920s, when a dollar was worth so much more than it is now.

The letter, which was part of a charitable campaign, appealed to people's goodwill. It asked recipients to return the dollar, and add more of their own, to help a hospital for crippled children. The letter offered a challenge, it pulled on the heartstrings, but most important, it got readers' attention with that crisp currency. Collier claimed it pulled a response rate better than 90 percent, a rate not often seen back then—or now. The same method of pinning money to a letter was used successfully at the time in a number of other applications, specifically to sell magazines. Once you have people's attention, there's no limit to what you can sell them.

Lewis Kleid, a contemporary of Collier who was a direct mail expert and list industry pioneer from Mailings Inc. in New York, wrote a series of direct mail newsletters at the time that were filled with instruction and information to help businesses plan their own campaigns. He titled one of the newsletters in the series

"Showmanship." In it, he said, "No matter how well you maintain the mailing list and prepare copy—it's all wasted if your message isn't ready when it reaches your prospect's desk."

He then suggested a number of different gimmicks that could be pasted, tied, stapled, or clipped to letters. The purpose of including them was to attract attention and make sure the letter would be kept at the top of the desk instead of being buried under a pile of other bland envelopes. It was necessary to find a way to keep the letter out in the open, where it had a chance of being read and therefore getting results.

Not only would these highly noticeable letters have a better chance of being read by the recipient, but it was also likely they would be shown to others. If the tie-in between the gimmick and the main idea of the letter was clever enough, it would help the reader remember the idea and maybe even lead him to talk about it to friends, who would spread the word about the product even farther.

It seems that back in the 1920s and 1930s, advertisers went to a lot of trouble to put together lumpy mail packages. Collier mentioned one magazine publisher who attached a wedding ring to his subscription renewal letters, requesting that the recipient not allow the lapsing subscription to go so far as a "divorce." Another magazine sent two aspirin tablets, saying that with all the "screwball madness of this world," the common sense and wisdom of their magazine would help keep the recipient sane and on track.

One company that sold dental gold sent a "diamond" ring to its potential buyers, with the note: "Sorry—This is not a diamond. But it looks like a diamond, doesn't it? . . . But it's a substitute!" The letter then went on to talk about how important it was not to use substitute materials for dental gold, where "quality, durability, and performance play an important part in your professional life and reputation."

Additional examples Collier cited involved attaching pictures of elephants, enclosing a skeleton key, perfuming a letter, personalizing letters with recipients' names (wouldn't Collier love to see what modern technology allows us to do with this approach today, including PURLs—personal URLs leading to a personalized website?), the use of special fonts that made letters look as though they were handwritten (again, a common practice today), and more.

A Word of Caution

While he obviously saw the value in using methods like this in direct mail campaigns, Collier also cautioned that this approach should be used judiciously:

> The purpose of all such "stunts" is to attract the reader's attention and get him into your letter. But like all stunts, they must be handled in such a way that the reader's interest, when won, may be guided quickly to the main idea of the letter.
>
> A circular letter is like a door-to-door canvasser in that its most difficult job is to get a hearing. Gift offerings and stunts and unusual openings help in this.
>
> But the main job is still ahead—to sell your idea or your product to the reader. Your stunt may soften him up, just as the Fuller salesman's free brush may make his approach easier, but it makes all the other steps in selling nonetheless necessary.

Where Can You Use a Little Showmanship?

Even with all the technological advances in methods of communication, direct mail is still one of the most effective ways to make sales. And the methods Collier suggests are still widely used today.

I mentioned the term "lumpy mail" earlier. This refers to any mail package that feels bulky and includes something intriguing along with the sales letter. Many direct mailers have had great success with this kind of approach, and you may be surprised at the variety of items the post office will accept.

If you are a direct mailer, think about how you might incorporate a little showmanship into your package. The idea is to make your package stand out from the rest of the mail sitting on someone's desk or kitchen counter. Even using a different color envelope or putting an interesting picture on it can capture your prospects' attention and increase the open rate. Your carefully crafted letter will ultimately clinch the sale, but adding a little showmanship may help to attract initial interest.

But maybe you aren't a direct mailer. Maybe you do most of your promoting online, whether it's for a business, a nonprofit group, or some kind of blog you're trying to turn into a business venture. You definitely want to find a way to stand out from all the other bloggers and posters and emailers who are competing with you for the attention of your target audience.

If you work mostly online, showmanship might involve incorporating online videos into your web pages. Or you might put a GIF—an eye-catching, continuously repeating, moving image— into your banner ad. Consider offering free samples to get people to click through to your site. It can also be effective to use outrageous headlines and email subject lines. (We'll investigate these in more detail in Chapter 6.) The goal is to do something surprising to get your prospects' attention. The possibilities are endless.

As an online marketer, you also might incorporate showmanship in another way by getting the physical addresses of your buyers and site visitors so you can send them direct mail! This is known as multichannel marketing, and it's well-established as an extremely valuable method for boosting response rates and creating deeper relationships with your audience. Combining online and offline marketing so each medium supports the other is one of the most effective ways to run a campaign.

Many online marketers find that following up with a direct mail piece (maybe one incorporating showmanship with lumpy mail) can solidify relationships with buyers.

As an online marketer, you would do well to consider matching physical addresses to your email list and start sending targeted direct mail to your best customers. This enables you to take advantage of powerful forms of showmanship that you may now think are beyond you.

And many marketers find that using direct mail to drive prospects to a website also solidifies relationships and increases sales. Relationships that begin offline and move online have been shown to have a much higher "lifetime value"—buyers buy more and stay with you longer. This is due to the higher engagement in the initial offline promotion.

Multichannel marketing continues to prove its value. If you're marketing in just one channel, you're not making the most of your opportunities. Don't define yourself by only calling yourself an internet marketer or a direct mail marketer. Use showmanship in both online and offline marketing for the best results.

THE IDEAL SALES LETTER (OR ANY OTHER PROMOTIONAL MATERIAL)

Now let's look past what you've done to get the attention of your prospects and look to what you'll tell them once you have it. Again, this is information you can use whether you're writing direct mail sales pieces, authoring a blog, filling out a job application, or creating copy for your website.

If one of the greatest marketers of his time were to tell you what he considered the essential elements of a sales letter, wouldn't you listen to what he had to say? Well, that's exactly what Robert Collier provided for us. In the last chapter of *The Robert Collier Letter Book*, he summarized what he saw as the attributes of the ideal sales letter. Collier was a master psychologist, and since human psychology hasn't changed over the past century, the advice he offered back in the 1930s is still relevant. So let's take a peek at what Collier had to tell us so we can apply these proven principles to the promotional writing we do today—in whatever form it may take.

Give Them What They Really Want, or "What the Newspaper Editor Told the Cub Reporter"

Collier told the story of a newspaper editor advising a cub reporter who was being sent out to cover a wedding. The editor enumerated the qualities of the ideal wedding that would appeal to tabloid readers: a beautiful heiress eloping with the chauffeur, an irate father with a shotgun and a high-powered car, a smashup, a heroic rescue, and a nip-and-tuck finish. The editor advised the reporter to approach the current wedding with this ideal picture in mind, see how many of those dramatic elements he could find, and then build his story around them.

In the same way, Collier said, when writing a letter to sell a product, you should put yourself in the place of your prospective buyer and think of everything that person could desire in the perfect form of that product. Make a list of all the features of the ultimate ideal. Then, with that in mind, write your letter, focusing on as many of those features as possible.

How can you use this idea? Let's look at an example. Suppose you're writing a recipe blog for busy career people who don't have much time but want to eat healthy meals. What would the ideal recipe be for such an audience? It would have to be delicious (a key aspect of any recipe), it would have a minimal number of ingredients, it would be quick and easy to prepare, it would improve a person's attractiveness, and it would be healthy.

So, in describing your recipes, you would include as many of these features as possible. You might even highlight specific health benefits, such as it helps you maintain weight, it promotes muscle growth, or it leads to glowing skin. The idea is to make a list of what your audience wants, and then tell them how you will give it to them.

Build a Memorable Picture

Collier said to write your letter in the heat of enthusiasm as you keep your ideal product in mind. Then he advised to leave it alone for a day so it (and you) can cool down. The following day, go back and look at the letter with a more objective eye. Now you can cross out all the details and descriptions you cannot honestly apply to the product. Don't worry. You'll still have plenty left to say once you've crossed out the excess.

The idea of taking extra time to create your best work is also advised by other legends. Later in this book we'll look at Eugene Schwartz's secrets for writing great copy without writer's block— including his unusual use of an egg timer! Many writers today think they have to go into a cave and write 24/7 until they have something finished, but there's a better way to do it, and the masters knew it.

Collier reminded us of the old saying:

There is nothing you can say about a 50-cent cigar that you cannot say about a 5-cent one.

Physically, the two cigars can be described the same way; the differences are only a matter of degree. The difference in quality will bring a difference in the degree of pleasure or satisfaction the smoker will experience, but this is a difference in the mind of the smoker only. Who's to say that a poorer man might not get as much pleasure from his 5-cent cigar as a rich man does from his 50-cent cigar? The copywriter can paint an equivalent picture of enjoyment for each.

The job of the marketer is to create descriptions that will build the anticipation of pleasure in the mind's eye of the reader, based on the physical facts of the product. Collier advised never to exaggerate or the prospect will disbelieve the whole thing. Create an attractive picture that builds such a powerful desire for the product that obtaining it is worth more to prospects than any price they have to pay.

Collier also said it is not necessary to cram every last fact and argument about the product into the letter. You can always put additional points into stand-alone pieces such as a lift note—a smaller sales letter with special information included in the envelope with the bigger letter. The best strategy is to pick one critical point on which you think the sale is going to hang and build the letter around it. Add powerful images and arguments that illustrate and support that main argument. This will make your letter strong and cohesive, leaving a memorable idea in the mind of prospects, where it can guide their behavior.

Add a Sense of Urgency

This may seem like a no-brainer for most of us in marketing today, but it wasn't so obvious back in the early part of the 20th century. It was Collier who pointed it out as a critical element in all promotions.

Every promotion you send out into the world (online, through the mail, in newspapers or magazines, on TV or radio) has to include a call to action where you tell prospects what you want them to do— for example, buy the product. Just asking for the order is not enough, though. The ideal promotion provides a reason why the person must respond at once. It develops a sense of urgency or, as Collier put it, a "Sword of Damocles" hanging over the prospect's head.

Put a time limit on the offer, or explain that supplies are limited so it's first come, first served. Or maybe announce that a price increase will take effect on a specified date. Make it very clear that the opportunity in the offer will be absolutely lost if the prospect does not take action within the specified time period.

Get the Prospect into the Promotion Immediately

We've looked at several sales tactics that contribute to the ideal sales letter, but Collier said other factors could add to or detract from how well a letter worked. For example, there are things you can do to make sure the reader looks inside the envelope. One obvious technique from Collier's day was to put some great "teaser" copy on the outside of the envelope (or, if you're selling through email, in an irresistible subject line) to make the reader curious about what's inside.

Coming up with a really good teaser can sometimes be difficult. So another approach is to make the envelope so personal looking and attractive that the reader feels compelled to learn who it's from and what it's about. This is important if the person has received several mailings from you and would recognize this as a sales letter right away.

In direct mail, one way to make the envelope more appealing is to hide the name of the sender by using an address without a name or using an attractive insignia that's intriguing without being recognizable. You can also change up the style of envelope, its color, the way the address appears, etc. One method Collier suggested is frequently used today: he said to make the letter look important by imitating a Western Union telegraph envelope—although today you might want to make the envelope look like a priority letter or a FedEx.

With email, the more you can personalize, the better, and the same principle of changing things up is critical. How does your new email message differ from the ones sent previously?

Final Points of Collier Wisdom

▌ *The sales letter carries the day.* Collier said that ultimately, the most important factor in clinching a sale is the sales copy itself. So while you need a good envelope, and adding an order card or circular may help, it's the letter that carries the load. As he put it:

> *If you have not the stuff in it, it does not matter where else you have it. It will not do you much good.*

So to help you write great promotions, he suggested keeping an "idea file" with good starters, descriptions, closers, and pointers that you collect from other writers. The goal is not to copy them, but to use them for inspiration.

▌ *It's always about the prospect.* Collier said:

> *The point that sells your customer is not what your product is, but what it will do for him!*

This same point is often expressed by promoters today by saying you want to stress benefits, not features. For example, if you're selling memberships to a health club, don't go on and on about the machinery and equipment. Instead, stress how great prospects will feel after working out on that scientifically designed equipment, how good they'll look, how much more energy they'll have, and the many ways in which their lives will improve.

▮ *Keep things as positive as possible.* Collier said that since the letter will be putting ideas into your reader's head:

> *Be careful not to put in negative ones that you will have to take out again before you can make a sale.*

As you know, many advertisers today use scare tactics. Collier didn't believe in that. It's something you have to decide and test out for yourself, given your product and audience.

One essential rule is that if you use fear, make sure you take prospects from the fear to the solution quickly. This seems to be what many marketers today do. Some have great success keeping prospects in fear longer than others, but eventually you must provide the solution for people to buy.

Many successful video sales letters today contain some of the scariest scenarios you can imagine, but throughout the video there is hope that an ideal solution will be provided in the end. They are fear-based, but also hope-based enough to make people want to keep watching. We're not sure Collier would approve, but we're pretty sure he'd ask about the results, which would be the ultimate measure of success. Fear may work, but bring people along in a way that keeps up hope.

▮ *The length of the letter must fit the purpose.* How much copy do you need to make a sale? If all you want to do is get people to make further inquiries, a short and snappy letter will do nicely. But if you are trying to get someone to commit to a purchase, you need to provide enough information to make that decision. Collier said:

> *So tell your story, no matter how long or how short it may be, striving simply to keep it interesting.*

There you have it: words from the master on the components of the ideal sales letter. You can put them to good use regardless of what you're selling or what medium you're using.

THE ROLLS-ROYCE EFFECT

Now let's look at some secrets of creative salesmanship from David Ogilvy. He advised promoters to follow these four basic principles in creating their messages:

1. *Creative brilliance.* Marketers need to come up with brilliant concepts that not only catch their best targets' attention but also sell them on the product. He was a proponent of what was called the "big idea"—an unforgettable concept that captures the imagination of your audience and puts your product (or yourself) on the map.

2. *Research.* Ogilvy did not believe in "blowing smoke." His copy was meticulously based in fact, and he did careful research to uncover the one amazing fact about a product around which he could build an entire ad campaign.

3. *Actual results.* Ogilvy was a strong believer in judging the quality of an ad by its success at selling the product. Always test the outcome of an ad, and if it isn't selling, make whatever changes are necessary to make it work. This holds true for print ads, banner ads, job applications, blog posts, or whatever else it is you're putting out into the world.

4. *Professional discipline.* Advertising executives were not to be dabblers in the creative realm. They needed to hone their craft and develop programs to train the next generation of advertisers. Similarly, if you want to be successful at promoting something, through any medium, apply yourself to creating the best campaigns possible or you'll never achieve everything that's possible for you.

This last point is as true today as it was when it was written. Nobody becomes a phenomenon in any field without putting in the time and discipline. This is especially true when it comes to writing promotions—particularly today, when the field is so much more competitive.

Back in Ogilvy's day, there were not as many advertising outlets. But given the noise of today's advertising world, in Brian's words,

"Advertising opportunities are now infinite." We've gone from three TV channels to hundreds. There are more magazines than ever. And of course there's the internet, Facebook, and Google—and anyone with access to the internet can be an advertiser.

So to be a successful copywriter, not only do you have to put in the hours to learn how to write, but you also have to research more than ever to make sure that what you write stands out. If you don't take deep dives into a product and learn what makes it unique, you'll never rise above the noise.

Today people talk about commodity versus specialty. A commodity is an ordinary product. A specialty product has something about it that makes it unique and exclusive. A great ad writer can take a commodity product and make it stand out as a specialty product by showing what makes it different and better.

The trick is to find the story in the product, and that takes skill. Maybe you're selling a fish oil supplement. You can turn it into a specialty item by explaining, for example, that your fish oil comes from a unique kind of fish living deep in Icelandic waters, providing better Omega-3. Researching your product has always been important, but it's even more important today. With more competition and a more skeptical audience, you need great arguments to back every claim you make.

The Most Famous Headline in Advertising History

Ogilvy wrote many famous ads during his career, but the one that is said to have been the most famous headline in advertising history was the one he created for Rolls-Royce. The headline read:

> *At 60 miles an hour the loudest noise in this new Rolls-Royce comes from the electric clock.*

This groundbreaking ad illustrates all the principles that made Ogilvy's work stand out. The headline itself was a wonderful example of the "big idea." No one had ever seen a headline like that before. It intrigued people and pulled them in to read the rest of the ad.

The body of the ad was made up of 13 interesting facts that clearly explained why the Rolls-Royce was unique and why it was worth its sky-high price. And of course Ogilvy tested the ad in a number of venues before launching the nationwide campaign that ended up earning a place in advertising history.

You might think marketers just sit around waiting for inspiration, but that's not the way it actually works. In describing the process he used to write the Rolls-Royce ad, Ogilvy said he started out, as he always did, by doing his homework. He claimed this was a tedious but necessary process. Ogilvy said that as a marketer, you had to study the product and find out as much about it as you can. The more you know about a product, the more likely you are to come up with the big idea.

When he got the Rolls-Royce account, he spent three weeks reading about the car. In the process he came upon this statement from a Rolls-Royce engineer: "At 60 miles an hour, the loudest noise comes from the electric clock." That became the headline, which was followed by 607 words of factual copy. In a sense, Ogilvy didn't even write the world's most famous headline; he took it from a company report. But his genius was in recognizing the power of the statement to work as the lead-in to the ad. Of course, the rest of the ad pulled its weight too: 13 carefully crafted points that each raised and answered a question the reader might have. It even addressed the issue of price in a clever way, stating that the Bentley, manufactured by the same company, was exactly the same machine except for the grille and a much-reduced price. People could buy a Bentley if they "feel diffident about driving a Rolls-Royce." This would subtly appeal to Rolls-Royce buyers, who would never see themselves as being diffident about anything.

Lessons for Today's Promoters

I think Ogilvy brought a modern touch to advertising that really made his work stand out—and also made it tremendously effective. Many of the copywriters I work with do just as he said: they spend as much time as necessary researching before they ever start writing.

Very often the facts themselves lead to the big idea that will really sell the product. It's the perspiration of research that gives rise to the creative inspiration. Smart advertisers put this into practice. Brian told me about a company he works with that hires entry-level copywriters to spend the first year or two only doing research. They don't write one word of copy until after they master researching the subject area they're going to be working on. Ogilvy understood the value of this, and once again he was ahead of his time.

We should also remember to always deal in facts. Especially today, consumers are wary of empty claims that seem to have nothing to back them up. In promoting your product or service or yourself, be sure to provide fact after fact that explain why you're the best.

And of course, Ogilvy was a pioneer in claiming that testing is everything. That's the only way to arrive at the best ad, sales piece, website copy, or Facebook post that will get you the best results.

THE NUMBER-ONE RULE OF SUCCESS

Eugene Schwartz is another legend who provided us with great insight into creative salesmanship. As you'll recall, Schwartz originated from Butte, Montana. And even though he ended up in Manhattan, living a sophisticated life and amassing an extensive collection of modern American art, he considered his small-town upbringing to be fortunate and invaluable to his business success.

It was because of his early experiences that he understood the desires and interests of the vast majority of Americans, and he never stopped learning as much about them as he could. He said:

> *You cannot lose touch with the people of this country, no matter how successful or how potent you are. If you don't spend at least two hours a week finding out where your market is today, you are finished!*

For this reason, he read the *National Enquirer* every week and went to popular films—the blockbusters all America was watching. To write effective ad copy, he learned to "talk little, listen much." He would listen to cab drivers, waitresses, shopkeepers—everyone he met, so he could become familiar with the language they used and the kind of images that appealed to them.

Schwartz took the same approach with his clients. He didn't do the talking in an attempt to impress them. Instead, he would let a client talk on and on about his product while he sat there quietly taking notes. He didn't see the copywriter as a creative genius. He didn't have to. As Schwartz put it:

You don't have to have great ideas if you hear great ideas.

Listening to the client is essential, or else the writer relies too much on his own creativity, which Schwartz thought was the kiss of death when it came to writing copy that worked.

Schwartz told the story of meeting with Marty Edelston, the founder of Boardroom Inc. Edelston had just $3,500 in his pocket at the time, and Schwartz warned him his fee was $2,500. Edelston was happy to pay it, so Schwartz just let Edelston talk about his vision for the newsletter he wanted to create. He talked for four hours while Schwartz took notes, and one point in particular caught his ear. The copy Schwartz ended up producing was 70 percent made up of what Edelston had said. And the headline was based on that one point Edelston made that caught his attention:

Now! Read 300 Business Magazines in 30 Minutes!
And Get the Guts of Every One of Their Most
Valuable Ideas—in Super Condensed Form
You Just Can't Forget!

That headline was the beginning of a multimillion-dollar business, and Schwartz didn't even make it up himself. It was Edelston's idea. Schwartz just picked up on it, wrote it out, and put it in a form where people would read it. The lesson is that you don't have to be creative. You just have to be in touch with your market, know your prospects, listen, and "let the ideas come to you."

Whether you're the business owner or the copywriter, it's important to share everything you know with each other. Don't leave anything out—miss no opportunity for additional insights. All that is needed is to get the person you're working with talking, just like

Schwartz did with Edelston. If Eugene Schwartz, the best copywriter of all time, said his clients wrote his best copy for him, you should be using the same method today.

The Secret of Success . . .

Schwartz made it very clear:

> *The number-one rule of success in anything—marketing, football, chess, etc.—is work.*

And Schwartz himself lived by that rule. Schwartz worked every day, including Saturdays and Sundays. Remarkably, he claimed to never have had writer's block. He created 12 to 15 mailing pieces a year and never had any problems getting started on them. (We'll look at exactly how he accomplished this in Chapter 7.) He worked from three to four hours every day, in half-hour spurts. With his method he had an 85 percent hit ratio, which meant that 85 percent of his ads paid out.

Schwartz said he got better results than many great copywriters—people who he knew were actually better writers than he was—because he worked harder than they did. His advice to anyone trying to succeed was to work harder than anyone else. He said that a brilliant writer who worked just a little would have a lower success rate than a cub writer who worked and worked and worked.

The reason for that was, as he believed, real creativity is not in the writer:

> *The creativity is in your market and in your product, and all you are doing is joining the two together.*

The writer's job is to dig out the nuggets he gets from listening to his client and then make the necessary connections. Another task is to find those hidden desires that motivate people—the things people don't like to talk about but that emerge in the culture and the subconscious.

A copywriter has to find out what prospects really want. During Schwartz's time, one of the best ways to learn the "extent of people's" ability to believe" was by reading popular magazines—even those crazy rags in the supermarket. Today all you have to do is click on one of the popular news sites, and you'll get all the information you need. Your best research on the hidden desires of your prospects is only a mouse click away.

Schwartz felt that the client had invaluable information about the hidden desires that would make people want to buy their product. He said that when working on a project, the writer should go to the person who created the product and listen. One way to do this was by reading anything the client might have written about it, and then talking to them while recording the conversation. You could pick up great ideas just by listening. All you had to do was get them talking.

By researching and listening, writers can end up knowing their products to the core—better than anyone else. This is also how they can find out what their products' sales appeal is. Then, using the images and language they've learned by listening to people on the street, they can string together what they know into winning promotional material.

This advice is for professional writers creating copy for someone else. If you're writing for your own promotions, have a brainstorming session with yourself. Again, don't make things up. Really work to come up with lists of the true benefits of what you do or what you make and anything that makes it stand out.

You must write copy by yourself, but once you have a draft written, you need to present it to others you trust. Make sure you have reliable sounding boards—people who will tell you the truth about how you are presenting your product or service. This is one reason why mastermind groups are so popular today. They provide an ideal opportunity for people to exchange creative ideas. You shouldn't write your copy by committee, but the best copywriters have a group of fellow marketers and copywriters around them who understand their market as well as they do, and they run their work by each other to see if there are any flaws.

As a final note, spend time thinking about your target audience and how what you do will help them. Even better, get in touch with members of your target audience and learn directly from them what they're looking for and what they like (and don't like) about your product. Be objective. Take notes. This is how you will unearth the nuggets that will put you on the map.

SELLING CREATIVELY

We've just seen a variety of ideas from our legends on creative salesmanship. Let's summarize some of the main points.

Get Your Prospects' Attention

This means using a little showmanship. Make yourself stand out from the crowd, and use some tricks to do it. If you're sending something through the mail, use teaser copy, a bright envelope, or even some kind of lumpy mail—all with the goal of getting your piece noticed, opened, and read.

If you'd like to learn more about the possibilities of lumpy mail, visit my website, TheAdvertisingSolution.com, and read my article "A New Dimension in Direct Marketing Success."

If you're promoting yourself or products online, use subject lines, headlines, videos, free offers—anything that will get people to take notice. One technique that's being used quite a bit now is to send an email or place small ads online linking to a letter with audio and video components. And even if you primarily promote online, think about showmanship ideas you can use offline with your best customers. It's all showmanship, and showmanship sells.

Use Key Elements for Every Promotion/Sales Letter

We also looked at elements you should include in your sales copy. Picture the ideal product, and then try to describe your product including as many of these ideal points as possible. Build anticipation in your prospects as you describe all the benefits they'll experience when they buy what you're selling. And add a sense of urgency so prospects feel the need to respond right away or they're going to miss out.

Make the Idea Big

Try to come up with a brilliant "big idea" that will really capture the imagination of your prospects, but don't feel you have to create that idea yourself. In fact, you shouldn't. Both Ogilvy and Schwartz taught that as you get more and more information about the product you're selling, the big idea will begin to emerge. Learn about your product. Talk to people who use it to find out what they want from it. Then use this research as the basis of your promotions.

Do the Work

Finally, do the necessary work. Don't cut corners. Talk to people. Find out what they want. Research your product. Learn what makes it unique. Spend time with your pen and paper or at your computer, so the creative juices can flow. You'll learn more about what to do throughout this book. There's no reason why you can't become a legend in your own niche.

CHAPTER 3

THE PSYCHOLOGY THAT SELLS

COUNTLESS PRODUCTS AND SERVICES are being offered for sale 24 hours a day. There are innumerable media through which all these things are being sold, including direct mail, magazine and newspaper ads, television ads, online ads, campaign speeches, blogs—even one-on-one sales pitches by employees at the local electronics store or car dealership. And what is a job application if not an opportunity to package and sell ourselves as attractively as possible?

Whatever you're selling—and whatever the medium—there is one constant that's critical to the success of any advertisement or promotion; one constant you have to be more aware of than any other aspect of your presentation. That constant is the psychology of the people you're trying to sell to. You have to understand the psychology of your prospects, and then present yourself or your product based on that understanding. These are the questions that have intrigued marketers since the beginning of civilization:

- ▮ What is it that appeals to people?
- ▮ What captures their attention?
- ▮ What motivates them to take action?
- ▮ What do you have to do to get them to buy what you're selling?

These are the very issues that the classic copywriters—our legends—understood so well. Their ability to use their knowledge of human psychology to create winning marketing campaigns accounted for much of their success. That meant being able to see the world not just from the marketer's perspective, but from the point of view of the people who had to be persuaded to buy the product.

These marketers may not have had formal training as psychologists, but they all used principles of psychology to achieve their aims. The two legends who best articulated their understanding of human psychology and how to use it to influence the behavior of their prospects were Robert Collier and Eugene Schwartz. They will be the focus of our study here. What you learn from them will be invaluable, regardless of the medium you use to reach your prospects.

IF YOU'RE GOING FISHING, YOU NEED BAIT

Robert Collier was an author of self-help and metaphysical books, as well as an advertising executive, so it is not surprising that in developing his promotions, he started not with the product he was selling but with trying to understand the person to whom he would be selling it. He was interested in the prospect's psychology.

In his classic treatise on writing sales pieces, *The Robert Collier Letter Book*, he opened with the question:

What is there about some letters that makes them so much more effective than others?

He concluded that it wasn't their finished style, their diction (that is, their use of language), or their adherence to rules. The answer lay in something so basic, it is expressed in the simple fishing parable that follows.

The Secret to Advertising—in a Fish Story

Collier asked us to consider two people who are fishing off a dock. One is a sophisticated sportsman, decked out with all the latest equipment. The other is a ragged urchin holding a branch with a string tied to it. (This was probably a more common sight in the 1920s than it is today.) The frustrated sportsman is having no luck at all, not even a bite, but the urchin is pulling in fish after fish. Why the difference?

Collier explained that it all comes down to the bait they're using. The boy knows what the fish will bite on, and that's what he gives them. The clueless sportsman is using high-tech lures that aren't fooling anyone—least of all the fish.

Collier said that with all the books written on fishing over many years, their main idea could be boiled down to one simple issue: "What bait will they bite on?" He believed the same principle worked when it came to creating promotional materials. To succeed, you had to understand the prospect. As he put it, you had to know:

> What is the bait that will tempt your reader? How can you tie up the thing you have to offer with that bait?

Collier understood the importance of building on the fact that we all want something. Whether conscious or unconscious, that desire is uppermost in our mind. It directs our interest and determines what will appeal to us.

The art of the marketer is to discern that desire and prepare a sales message that somehow ties together that desire with the product being advertised so readers feel certain that obtaining that object will get them closer to fulfilling their desire—or that *not* obtaining it will make it more difficult to fulfill that desire.

Doing this requires that you, the developer of the sales material, know your prospects' deepest wishes and how to appeal to them.

You also have to understand certain things about human nature so you can approach your prospects the right way.

The Right Approach

Collier asked marketers to put themselves in the place of their prospects. For example, he asked us to imagine that we were deep in conversation with a friend about something that was very important to us. Along comes a stranger who slaps one of us on the back and tells us he has a coat he wants to sell us. Would we drop everything and examine the coat? Or would we push him away as an annoyance? Probably the latter.

It's the same when a prospect receives a sales letter or comes upon any other kind of promotion. He is (and this is one of those remarkable insights Collier drops throughout his books):

> . . . *deep in a discussion with himself over ways and means of getting certain things that mean a great deal to him.*

It's true. We're always thinking about the subject that interests us the most—ourselves! We're reliving a past event, or imagining something in the future that either tempts or frightens us. In effect, for prospects, your message barges in and tells them to stop thinking about what they want to think about, and start thinking about what you want them to think about. We can't assume their response will be favorable.

Is there another way to approach prospects that will get a better result? There is, and it's to make your message more about them and less about you.

Going back to the coat salesman, a better approach would be to hang back, listen to the dialogue, get the feel of it, and then ease into the conversation on a related topic. Once engaged, he could gradually bring the discussion around in logical increments until what he wanted to talk about seemed like the perfect next step.

It's the same with preparing any promotional material—for example, writing a sales letter, an email, or a banner ad. There are certain thoughts that are generally part of the deep discussion people have with themselves. This is where the marketer starts breaking into the inner conversation to get the prospect's attention. This is the bait.

But every species of fish requires a different kind of bait. So marketers must study their prospects to:

Find a point of contact with his interests, his desires, some feature that will flag his attention and make your letter stand out from all the others the moment he reads the first line.

A letter selling a baby stroller to a new mother might start by appealing to her love of her baby. It would then move on to how that precious baby deserves every advantage, including a new baby stroller, in which he will be admired by the world as he should be.

A letter (or website copy) selling insurance against burglary and theft to a homeowner might start by talking about the increase in crime, giving the scary statistics, and then saying that a good insurance policy is a cheap investment to protect all that is near and dear to him.

Collier concluded that whatever you are selling, you have to start with the right bait:

Find the thing your prospect is interested in and make it your point of contact, instead of rushing in and trying to tell him something about your proposition, your goods, your interests.

First written in 1931, Collier's words still hold powerful lessons for us. Successful advertising is not about the product. It's about the prospect. Learn and understand what your prospect wants, and build your campaign around that. It really is timeless wisdom about human nature and motivations.

WHEN IT COMES TO EVERY KIND OF MARKETING, EMOTIONS PAY!

Collier's insights into human nature and how he used them to manipulate interest in his products are of tremendous practical use to marketers today. Let's look deeper at what Collier had to say about emotions and motivation. Understanding Collier's take on these two qualities can help us increase our effectiveness at reaching prospects.

Emotion

Collier said that before you start writing a sales letter (and you can insert here any other kind of promotional material), you have to ask yourself what emotion you want to arouse in your reader. The purpose of arousing that emotion would be in the service of fulfilling your primary goal: to make readers want to do what you are asking them to do.

You must bring readers to the point where they feel they must do what you want and that they won't be able to rest easy until they have taken the action you propose. A sales proposition that just aims at the intellect won't do the trick. It is missing the motivating element. You have to go for the emotions if you're going to inspire readers to take action. What kind of emotions are we talking about?

- ▮ *Love.* To be successful, you don't just sell a child's bicycle. You sell a bicycle that will bring joy and confidence to a beloved child.
- ▮ *Shame.* Don't just sell a box of greeting cards because they'll be convenient to have on hand when you need one. Sell a box of cards that will enable readers to keep up with all those acquaintances they feel guilty about ignoring for so long.
- ▮ *Vanity.* You might sell some face cream by describing all its scientifically tested natural moisturizing ingredients. However, you'll sell a lot more by saying the cream will make the reader look ten years younger, all her friends will be envious of her youthful appearance, and her husband will fall in love with her all over again.

This quote from Collier says it all:

Appeal to the reason, by all means. Give people a logical excuse for buying that they can tell to their friends and use to salve their own consciences. But if you want to sell goods, if you want action of any kind, base your real urge upon some primary emotion!

It may sound cynical, but if you really believe in your product or service, you will see the truth and the value in it. You know what you're offering will improve your prospects' lives. It's your job to convince them of that fact. That means you have to find the right emotion and build your appeal around that.

Emotion over Facts

For example, if you're a dentist, just listing all your degrees, saying you use advanced techniques, and boasting about your newly appointed office will not necessarily get people to try your services. One emotion that keeps people from going to the dentist is fear, and that would be an excellent issue for you to address.

So you might describe how you specialize in painless techniques and that your patient rooms are designed with comfortable chairs, earphones, heated blankets, and every amenity to allay anxiety—all of which speaks directly to their fear and everything you do to relieve it.

Another emotion that works to get people to the dentist is vanity. We all know how unappealing a set of poorly maintained teeth can be. So you could play up the embarrassment people feel when their teeth don't look right by showing before-and-after pictures of people who have used your service and now feel so much more attractive and confident.

Think of the emotions (and motivations) that will get people to buy your product or service, and use those as the basis of your sales message.

Motivation

"Exercising persuasion" is Collier's notion that we must understand the motives that make people buy. Again, his direct way of explaining what he meant is worth repeating:

What is persuasion? Nothing but finding the motive that will impel your reader to do as you wish, then stirring it to the point where it is stronger than his inertia, or his economical tendencies.

Collier advised letter writers to put themselves in the place of their readers and try to determine the prospects' prime motivating factors (rather than considering what would motivate the letter writer personally). In Collier's experience, there were six basic motivations underpinning human behavior:

1. Love
2. Gain
3. Duty
4. Pride
5. Self-indulgence
6. Self-preservation

These motivations often occur in combination. So prospects might be motivated primarily by pride when considering buying a new car, but to appeal to pride alone would be too limited. You should throw in a dash of love (it will be safer for your family), gain (you'll be saving a fortune on repairing your old clunker), and of course some self-indulgence (you'll feel like royalty with all the luxury features of the new car).

In preparing your sales material, you'll need to turn that motivation into a spur to make your prospect take action right away. The old car is putting the family in immediate danger; the special reduced price will only be available for a limited time; driving the old clunker diminishes the reader in the eyes of neighbors and friends every day.

Make it clear what readers have to gain by taking immediate action and what they could potentially lose if they don't. You build their desire to act by showing them how their lives will be improved by doing what you say. Spell it out very clearly so they are impelled to act.

Going back to our dentist, you might explain to readers that taking care of their teeth will improve their health and well-being in many areas: unattractive teeth are holding them back from professional success and are hurting their relationships; the cost of good dental maintenance now will save them money and pain down the line; and by taking advantage of your special assessment and cleaning for new patients—available only for a limited time—they can get started on a new program of health for the entire family, at a very reasonable cost. This is the best time to get started on a healthy future.

To quote Collier again:

> *Bring home to him the advantages that will accrue to him from doing as you wish, in so effective a way that he wants these more than anything of any trouble they may cost him.*

These basic rules for selling effectively are eternal. I'm sure the vendors hawking products in the bazaars of ancient Mesopotamia used these same principles. Collier just showed how to adapt these rules to creating sales letters and promotional materials that really work—and that still work today.

THE CHIMPANZEE BRAIN

Eugene Schwartz conveyed many of the same ideas that Collier did, only he seemed a little less tactful in his descriptions of human nature. As Schwartz put it, we human beings all think we're rational. We believe all our decisions are based on logic, and we can provide a good explanation for everything we do. Yes, other people often seem to act without rhyme or reason, but we always know why we do things, and it always makes perfect sense. And when it comes to being manipulated by others, we would never fall for emotional arguments. You can't slip anything by us.

Or so we'd like to believe.

Eugene Schwartz didn't buy it. He saw through all those flattering self-images, all the way down to the deeper motivations that underlie so many of our decisions and actions. Schwartz's interpretation of brain science is that there are three levels to our brain physiology and function, from low to high:

1. The reptilian brain, or the basal ganglia
2. The paleomammalian brain, or the limbic system
3. The neomammalian brain, or the cerebrum

Each of these brain levels serves an important role in our survival. According to this theory, we primarily function from the higher brain level, but the lower levels of our brain are always operating. Schwartz described the role of the lower brain centers in a unique way, calling the part of us that looks out at the world and makes our decisions for us our "chimpanzee brain."

According to Schwartz, human beings are simply a more advanced chimpanzee that made its first appearance several hundred thousand years ago. That's nothing compared to the timeline of the planet and even the timeline of mammals on earth. These older parts of our psyche are well-established and barely overridden by the human intellect.

So here we are, whiling away time by reading a magazine, or watching TV, or surfing the internet. We're not really paying much attention, but if someone were to interrupt us and ask what we're doing, we would answer that we're functioning from our logical cerebrum. You have to wonder about that when you see some of the stuff that goes viral on the internet these days. But even so, we each think we're the exception.

When we read advertising, op-ed articles, or blogs, we feel as though writers are speaking to that higher part of our brains so we can believe that's the part that makes the decisions. But in fact, Schwartz said, it's that lower part of us that's peeking out and doing the reading. We think we're working with the cerebrum, but it's the reptilian brain that's actually reacting and deciding.

This poses something of a challenge for the writer, who must find a way to appeal to both parts of the brain. For example, suppose a man feels he's always struggling with money. He doesn't have any plan for dealing with his problem, but one day he gets a direct mail piece or sees an online ad about a course he can buy that will teach him a method of investing. His chimpanzee brain loves the idea of making scads of money quickly without doing any work, but his human brain knows logically that no program can possibly provide that.

If he sees the headline "Get Five Million Dollars Dropped on Your Doorstep Without Lifting a Finger," that might appeal to his chimpanzee brain, but it will never get past the censor in his cerebrum. The human brain will know it's ridiculous and toss the sales piece aside without even reading it.

So, if you're the writer, you know you have to come up with something that sounds reasonable to the human brain but still appeals to the chimpanzee brain. If you can strike the right balance in your copy, the prospect will go for it.

As Schwartz described the prospect's thought processes:

Now, he's going to look for the best, most rational, and most honest approach possible. But he's also going to have that little sly side of him, and you are going to have to appeal to that to sell to him.

You need to run a covert operation where you appeal to both levels. So you might come up with a headline like this:

Here's How My Daily Market Reports Could Have
Helped You Profit More Than $34,291 in
Less Than Four Months.

We discuss the basics of a great headline in Chapter 6, but let's look at how a headline like this talks to both sides of the brain at the same time.

The cerebrum sees a reasonable-sounding promise. There's nothing extreme here. It's a lot of money for most people, but it's not a ludicrous amount. It makes it sound like the reader could have made a nice amount of money in a realistic period of time. And the headline assures that the reader won't be learning and working alone—an expert will be helping out.

Using such a specific dollar amount and precise time period adds credibility to the claim. It doesn't seem likely that someone would make up such odd-sounding numbers. (And in fact, the claim would have to be accurate or the advertiser could be in trouble.) Many readers perceive detailed promises like this as carrying more weight, making the whole program worth learning more about. So they start reading the rest of the sales piece.

But there's more going on here than meets the eye. Because while the cerebrum is being distracted by the "reasonableness" of the headline, the chimpanzee brain receives the hidden message and thinks, "I can make a lot of money from someone else's work. Sounds great!"

Appealing to both sides of the brain is critical for success. Today you hear horror stories of people getting huge front-end responses to their promotions online, but then no one converts into a buyer, no one renews, or return rates are high. The problem is the product could never live up to the overblown promise.

Here's a word to the wise: It's understandable that you're trying to get people's attention through all the noise. But if you make the claims too outrageous, even if you get a high front-end response, you'll pay on the back end. The promoters who get buyers who stay the longest and have the greatest lifetime value are the ones who appeal to both parts of the brain.

You might think you have the right balance, but if there's too much appeal to the chimpanzee and not enough to the human, you'll see it in high returns and low retention. The longer-term metrics don't lie.

Hidden Desires

So what is the chimpanzee looking for that you have to hint at in your promotional material? An important task of the successful marketer, in Schwartz's words, is to "find those hidden desires" that motivate people. Often those desires are hidden from the prospects themselves.

The chimpanzee desires remain unknown and unacknowledged by the cerebrum, but they still direct behavior. These hidden desires include things people don't like to talk about or don't want to recognize in themselves, but they give themselves away by cropping up in popular culture.

As we saw in Chapter 2, Schwartz said one way the writer can find out what prospects really want is to read popular magazines, even celebrity gossip magazines in the supermarket. Of course, today we have another amazing source of this information that Schwartz wasn't privy to—the internet. There's a world of information in all those wild online stories that people tell themselves they only click on out of idle curiosity.

When people read these stories, they may do it with a sense of superiority, but these articles actually touch on hidden desires, which is why people click on them in the first place. It's that chimpanzee brain being curious, wondering, "What's in it for me?"

So look at what's being talked about on the internet or any other form of popular culture. As Schwartz put it, this is how you can find out the "extent of people's ability to believe." The insight you get into the way people's minds work can be invaluable in creating highly effective promotional pieces.

"Who Are You Writing To?"

Another important aspect of creating promotions that really work is to understand exactly who your audience is. Schwartz explained:

> *You are not writing to a private person. You are not writing to a bunch of people. You are writing to a number of people who share a private want. . . . And you are addressing them as if they were the only person in the world.*

Schwartz declared that the most powerful word in advertising is not "free!" It's "you!"

Of course, even though you're talking to a group of people who share a private want, not all those people will be exactly the same. They have different qualities and experiences, and therefore have to be approached in different ways.

For example, suppose you are selling some kind of health supplement that claims to relieve arthritis pain. You have some potential buyers who are athletic men who have been slowed by arthritis as they've gotten older. You also have some potential buyers who are pretty women who have been popular all their lives and who now don't feel quite as attractive as they once did. These different groups both fear losing their sense of who they are, but they share subsections of that want.

So you need to appeal to these different subsections with different "hooks" that you sprinkle throughout the piece. For the men, you might hint at regaining the power that they have been watching slip away. They will be fierce competitors once again! For the women, you might talk about going dancing with their husbands and once again feeling attractive and cherished.

You may pick up 5 percent of your prospects with one hook and 10 percent with another. By speaking to the specific wants of each group, you can keep each of the subsections interested and reading. However, in order to speak to those specific wants, you have to first find out what they are. You have to understand the psychology of the people you want to sell to.

Channel Demand

Given Schwartz's organic approach to writing his sales pieces, in which he allowed the needs of his prospects to determine the direction of the piece, his next point makes perfect sense:

You don't create demand for whatever it is you're promoting.

It's impossible to create demand where it doesn't exist. The demand already has to be out there. The marketer's job is simply to identify that existing demand and then focus it on the product being sold, presenting it as the answer to that demand.

To be successful, you have to know your prospects. Find out what they want, what motivates them, what their concerns are. Then take that existing demand and call upon it in your ad copy. Create a piece that focuses not on what the product is, but on what it does to meet that demand.

This is important for anyone who is trying to influence behavior. If you're a shop owner, you need to know what your customers are really after. Then speak to those desires in your advertising, in the way you dress your windows, and in the way you lay out your store. For example, dry cleaning isn't exciting, but appearing professional and successful in beautifully pressed clothing is. Exercising can be boring, but meeting other people at the gym and getting a ripped body can be very appealing.

If you're a blogger, write your blog based on the desires of your best prospects. Whether you're providing recipes for busy women or giving golf tips to amateur golfers, don't just provide information. Find out what people really want and what their deeper motivations are, and then make sure you address those issues directly in what you write.

Maybe the busy woman feels guilty she's not spending enough time with her children. Give her easy, child-pleasing recipes that everyone can make together. Promise her that if she does what you suggest, she will feel like a Supermom! Similarly, golfers often feel frustrated because they never know what kind of game they'll play from one day to the next. If they play a bad game, it can embarrass them in front of their golfing buddies—and often, the more they worry about it, the worse it gets. Promise them authority, confidence, and the ability to outplay everyone else. Make them believe that with your help they'll be the alpha golfer. But don't say it in so many words. Hint at it. Speak to the cerebrum and the chimpanzee brain at the same time.

HOW TO SELL WITH EMOTION

Let's go back to Collier now, because his phenomenal success as a copywriter made him a figure that many ad writers and promoters still turn to for advice and inspiration. In *The Robert Collier Letter Book*, he dissected a series of ads to show what made them succeed or fail. It's like a graduate course in how to use psychology to prepare effective promotions.

One of the chapters in his book, "How to Arouse That Acquisitive Feeling," analyzed ads for the degree of emotion they were able to provoke in people. As mentioned earlier, Collier believed (and proved again and again in his own work) that ads that touched readers' emotions were more successful than ads that only touched the intellect.

You can provide a ton of arguments to convince the intellect of the advantage of making a certain choice, but unless you make readers feel that they have to have what you offer and that it will be worth any effort to get it, your sales letter will be worthless. To use Schwartz's terminology, you have to appeal to that chimpanzee brain.

Collier advised that before writers put even one word down on paper, they need to decide what effect they want to have on the reader. They have to know the feeling they need to arouse so the prospect will be moved to take action. The point of the ad is not to make the reader think, "What a clever ad." Rather, it is to arouse in readers the feeling of "Let's go!"

To recap what both Schwartz and Collier have been telling us, marketers must determine what feeling has to be aroused to lead prospects to take action. From there, they must consider what kind of argument should be presented to inspire that feeling in readers so that taking action will become irresistible. As Collier put it:

> *Isn't the prime requisite arousing in your reader the feeling that he must have the thing you are offering, or that he cannot rest until he has done the thing you are urging him to do?*

Of course, people don't want to feel as though their emotions are being manipulated. They want to believe they're making decisions based on logic (i.e., you have to placate that good old cerebrum). The challenge of the writer is to present arguments that seem to convince the intellect, while in fact aiming at their emotions.

Collier gives two examples. The first letter had only moderate success, while the second letter pulled more than twice as many responses. Both letters sold boxes of greeting cards, and while the first presented some sound intellectual arguments, the second went straight for the emotions. You can see the difference right in their opening paragraphs:

Letter One—Intellectual Appeal:

Some people have a sort of sixth sense that enables them to send greetings and the like to all the proper relatives and friends on every appropriate occasion. But most of us are likely to overlook such things.

Compare that to the opening paragraph of the second letter:

Letter Two—Emotional Appeal:

How often have you promised yourself to keep in touch with some old friend, to cultivate some new one—and then gone your way forgetting them, and letting them forget you?

The second letter immediately brings up the image of a potential loss readers could experience if they don't follow up on the offer. It's that twinge of guilt and loss that keeps the reader going to the next paragraph and the next to learn how to resolve those unpleasant feelings. It primes them to take the easy solution the letter is about to offer.

The goal of either of these letters is to get readers to place orders for personally inscribed cards so they can get them back in time for Christmas. Let's look at the final two paragraphs of each letter.

Letter One—Intellectual Appeal:

The time is getting close now. It won't be long before you will be wanting to mail these cards. Better fill in your name now on the payment blank—tell us how many more cards to send you, and drop it in the mail.

Then the days may come and days may go, but you'll be sure of having attractive greetings with which to keep green all your friendships.

Letter Two—Emotional Appeal:

And of all ways to recall yourself to your absent friends, none is more pleasant or easier than sending them a lovely

Christmas greeting, like the box of fifteen that we mailed to you a short time ago, for they are not only good to look at, but they carry with them a warm-hearted greeting that every friend will welcome.

Remember, it is not the intrinsic value of what you send that counts. It is the spirit that goes with it. As Oliver Wendell Holmes put it, "If uncounted wealth were thine, thou couldn't not to thy cherished friends a gift so dear impart, as the earnest benediction of a deeply loving heart.

Granted, quoting Oliver Wendell Holmes wouldn't get you very far today, but it worked well in Collier's time. The specific words aside, this letter worked because it touched on people's emotions.

It takes a lot to get people over their inertia, and it takes a lot to get them to consider spending money on anything. Even motivating people to click through to your website takes effort. You have to convince your prospects that they will feel so much better as a result of buying your product—that they will feel so much better about themselves.

For example, most people know that eating healthy food is good for them, but if you want them to come to your store and stock up on beet juice, you have to play upon their guilt, fear, and vanity. So when they come into your store to look through your line of supplements, don't just talk about the pristine way a certain brand of vitamins is processed. Talk about how much better they'll feel, how their doctors will be impressed by their healthier numbers, and how great they'll look.

Here's another example. People may think it would be nice to have a lot of money, but if you want them to buy your course on investing in stock options, you have to paint a picture of how secure they'll feel when their money problems are over forever, when they can supply their loved ones with everything they want and need, and when they feel the pride of accomplishment as they look at their bank balance. Of course, keep assuring them how easy and stress-free the learning process will be.

People may also know it's a good idea to cook balanced meals for their families, but if you want them to keep visiting your healthy-eating blog, add stories about family meals in your own home, the joy of cooking together, and funny or heartwarming experiences sent in by other readers. Make reading your blog an emotional experience, not just a list of ingredients and directions.

Whatever you're selling, try to determine the main factors that impel people to take the action you want them to take, and then appeal to those factors while keeping the intellect happy with arguments that satisfy it. To repeat Collier's classic quote:

Appeal to the reason, by all means. Give people a logical excuse for buying that they can tell to their friends and use to salve their own consciences. But if you want to sell goods, if you want action of any kind, base your real urge upon some primary emotion!

People have not changed since Collier wrote those words. We are just as emotional as ever, and that is still the best way to reach your reader. As a marketer, a good place to start is with yourself. Ask yourself, "What would get me over my inertia so I would take action?"

You can begin with your own experience, but don't stop there. Your prospects may have different experiences and goals. You have to find out what your prospects want, so do some investigating. Talk to the people who are already your best buyers or who are buying things similar to what you want to sell them.

Many online marketers are using new survey products to learn more about potential prospects. The power of the internet allows them to get this important information from multiple people very quickly and act on it in meaningful ways. If you can't talk to people directly or survey them online, read the same magazines and online articles they do to find out what interests them. This will help you determine their "hidden desires" and find out what really motivates them to act.

The fact that a core premise of Schwartz's classic *Breakthrough Advertising* is finding "mass desire" is no accident. He would have used all the tools available today to determine this and use it to his full advantage.

CHAPTER 4

SECRETS OF WRITING GREAT COPY—PART I

W E'VE LOOKED AT DIFFERENT WAYS to make yourself stand out by using a little showmanship (Chapter 2) and how to use psychology to add to the effectiveness of your promotions (Chapter 3). In this chapter, we're going to dig deep into the nuts and bolts of creating ads in all media, offline and online. These are the mechanical laws of creating copy that is really effective at influencing people's behavior—and these laws have been around forever.

There's so much information to cover that we'll present it in two separate chapters. In this chapter, we'll concentrate on the wisdom of our two earliest legends: Claude Hopkins and Robert Collier.

HOPKINS' LAWS FOR WRITING COPY THAT SELLS

As we mentioned in Chapter 1, Claude Hopkins was a whiz at writing effective advertising copy in the early part of the 20th century, but what really made him stand out was that he tested everything before he presented it to the public. Just believing that your copy is good and then going ahead and using it is no way to run a business. As Hopkins knew from his own early industrial years, a manufacturer tests every aspect of his materials and processes. By the same token, he should test the effectiveness of his advertising copy.

As a result of the dedicated testing he did with his own copy, Hopkins knew for a fact what elements of copy worked and what didn't. Knowing this, he was able to apply his findings to all his new campaigns, so that he kept achieving better and better results. In his classic book, *My Life in Advertising*, Hopkins included a chapter on "Scientific Advertising," in which he laid out some of the basic laws of writing copy that sells, based on years of testing different ways of presenting his sales pitch and analyzing the resulting response rates.

Here are just some of these laws that worked back then—and still work today:

∎ *Brilliant writing has no place in advertising.* The novice copywriter writes to impress and makes the mistake of putting readers' attention on the copy, instead of on how the readers' lives will improve by using the product in question.

What good is it for people to comment on how beautifully the copy is written if it doesn't impel them to take action? Even today we see clever ads that people remember clearly, but they have no idea what product the ad was selling!

Hopkins believed that the less noticeable the copy, the better it will be at doing its job. All you need to do is present the facts and benefits and let them do the selling for you. It helps to be a little subtle. If the copy appears to be trying to persuade, the reader will reject it out of what Hopkins called "fear of over influence." Your copy should appear to inform readers so they think the decision to take action was all their own idea. Don't let the writing be conspicuous. As Hopkins put it:

> *In fishing for buyers, as in fishing for bass, one should not reveal the hook.*

▍ *Language should be natural and simple.* Remember your audience and write so they can understand you and feel that you understand them. Use the same language your audience uses. We see this idea expressed again and again by our legends.

Above all, you must be clear. If people have to struggle to get the message, they may miss it altogether; then you won't get any response at all. Lay it all out in logical steps, using language your audience is comfortable with.

▍ *Never try to show off.* The whole point of promotional material is to sell a product or an idea, not the writer. Sincerity, not fancy words, is called for. Trying to show off irrelevant knowledge will just put people off.

Of course, if you're presenting yourself as an expert on a certain subject, then by all means make it clear you're experienced and knowledgeable. But don't talk down to people. That won't bring you the results you want.

▍ *From start to finish, offer service.* Your prospects want to know what you will do for them. Anything that smacks of being self-serving or trying to manipulate their behavior will make them suspicious. Hopkins said he had seen many ads ruined by inserting phrases like "Insist on [this brand]" or "Avoid imitations." He believed these phrases hinted at a motive on the seller's part that was of no interest to the prospect. Tell prospects how they will benefit by buying from you or visiting your site or hiring you—what you can do to make their lives better—rather than warning them against buying from someone else.

▮ *Forget yourself entirely.* In putting together your sales copy, leave yourself out of the equation. Prospects don't care about you; they care about themselves. And that's why your focus should be on them. Imagine your prospect is standing before you, a specific individual, and think about what you would say to that person to convince him or her that getting their hands on your product would be a great thing for them personally. Picture what a good salesman, talking to the prospect around the kitchen table, would say. That's what you should say in your copy.

It's true that many companies will make a brand out of an individual and use that person as the basis of promotional materials, but they don't so much talk about the person and his or her accomplishments as they give the impression that readers can accomplish all that person achieved by using the product.

Of course, if you're looking for a job or a date, you probably will have to focus more on your specific qualities, but speak of them objectively and emphasize not so much how brilliant you are, but what a great addition you'd make to the company or to the other person's life.

▮ *Do not boast.* You may be tempted to say things like "Our operation is the largest in the country," but that's really of no interest to the prospect. It's just a boast, and as Hopkins reminds us, "Boasting is repulsive." Plus, what difference does it make if you're the biggest or the first? That doesn't tell people anything about how their lives will be better if they use your product.

Tell them how great they will be once they get their hands on your product, and how much effort you'll put in to make sure they're satisfied. That's really all they want to know. If they think you're too full of yourself, they may believe their satisfaction won't be all that important to you.

▮ *Aim to get action.* You have to put something in your ad that will inspire people to take action. One method is to include some kind of coupon that signals people they should place an order. This is especially useful in print ads, allowing them to clip out the coupon and keep it as a handy reminder.

This can also work well in direct mail ads. Even if your ad encourages people to call to place orders or visit a website, just seeing the coupon is a powerful cue to take action. If you're working online, you might use a picture of a coupon as a visual cue, but the real cue to take action is a link that prospects can click.

One of the benefits of working online is that you have great flexibility to place the link at different points in your email or web page. A link near the beginning can serve prospects who are convinced after the first few paragraphs. Other links can be placed throughout the piece, giving prospects an opportunity to act whenever they're ready.

As we mentioned earlier, one very effective way to get more prospects to take action is to approach them through different media. Brian likes to think of this as the concept "O . . . to O . . . to O": online to offline to online. The idea is to use multiple channels to get your message out. (I also talk about this concept in my book *The Direct Mail Solution*). For example, you might bring people to your website through a URL printed on a direct mail piece. Or perhaps they order from a catalog through an 800 number. In either case, your next goal is to obtain an email address.

Prospects are now brought into an online funnel from an offline medium. Research shows they will probably have a higher lifetime value because they came to you offline, which usually has much higher involvement and engagement from the prospect. And now that you've made the online connection, you can communicate with them much less expensively to get them to take further action.

Conversely, if you're running an online promotion, ideally you would get your prospects' physical addresses so you can send them something through direct mail, just as we talked about in Chapter 2. Now you can use many of the proven direct mail methods to get attention—and take action.

Take advantage of current technology to mix the way you communicate. Prospects today may actually enjoy being able to move across channels. It's certainly to your benefit. Of course, Hopkins didn't know the internet was coming, but I think he'd be excited about all these new possibilities to get action from the prospect, crisscrossing media, with the flow of traffic moving both ways in every channel.

▌ *Build urgency.* Speaking of encouraging action, limited-time offers are very effective. If people are afraid an offer will soon go away, it will give them a reason to act quickly. If they feel time is not an issue, they'll defer action until later, and more than likely, they will forget about it. Adding a sense of urgency increases response rates, and this should be carefully built into all your sales and promotional pieces.

▌ *Frivolity has no place in advertising.* Hopkins felt that advertising was serious business and should not include humor. For Hopkins, money represented life and work, and asking people to spend their hard-earned money should not be taken lightly. We must realize, however, that much of Hopkins' working life took place during the Depression, when money was indeed a very serious subject for many people. And let's not forget the influence of his thrifty "Scotch mother"!

For the most part, it's true: building an entire sales piece around humor is a mistake. First, it would grow old fast. Second, what one person considers funny may just seem weird or stupid—or even offensive—to someone else.

However, injecting a bit of humor may add something positive to a marketing piece. When it comes to humor, we should take a cue from Hopkins and test it out. If you have an idea for something amusing, maybe a joke or a cartoon, use it and see if it improves response. If it does, great, but if it doesn't, be ruthless and cut it out.

Some writers find that adding an element of surprise or a bit of humor to sales copy can be effective at capturing and keeping attention. To learn more about it, visit my website at TheAdvertisingSolution.com and read my article "Surprise! The Value of Adding an Unexpected Element to Your Sales Copy."

█ *Ads should tell the full story.* Never assume your reader knows anything about you or has read another ad in a series. Each ad should be able to stand on its own. If you're sending out a sales piece followed by additional letters or emails, make sure you put all the important information in each piece, including your major arguments and bullet points. Perhaps later pieces can be pared down in size, but don't assume your reader will remember points he may have seen in earlier pieces.

Also realize if you put several different appeals in a single sales piece, some will work better with some prospects, while others will work better with different prospects. Make sure all the appeals are presented in every piece, or you could be losing prospects who might otherwise buy.

MORE OF HOPKINS' LAWS FOR WRITING COPY THAT SELLS

Now let's look at some more wisdom from Claude C. Hopkins, one of the greatest copywriters of his day. We just looked at some of his basic, proven principles, but he had a lot more to share. Here are some additional rules that worked for Hopkins in his day, which are still worth following today:

█ *Superlative claims don't count.* Your readers know you're trying to sell them something, and they don't put much value in claims like "The Best in the World." You're expected to exaggerate, so readers won't fault you for saying it, but it does nothing to advance your cause and it makes your readers put less stake in anything else you say. If one claim seems unreasonable, they may just discount all your other assertions.

What works better than such puffery are actual figures and facts that support the benefits of your product. Readers know advertisers cannot make misleading claims when it comes to facts. Since they figure you are unlikely to risk a lawsuit, you must be telling the truth.

The more specific the facts you give, the better. An indefinite claim leaves an indefinite impression. Hopkins gives the example of selling a tungsten lamp by claiming it's better than a coal lamp (which clearly shows how long ago he wrote the book!). If you just say the tungsten lamp gives more light, no one will be impressed. But if you tell them the tungsten lamp gives three-and-a-half times as much light as a coal lamp, people will be impressed and assume you're telling the truth. After all, who would make up such a specific fact? It gives the impression that it's based on actual testing.

So don't make broad, empty claims. It will devalue your entire promotional piece. Make a specific claim, and not only will people be more likely to take notice of it, but they will also look more favorably on the rest of your statements.

▌ *Never advertise negatively.* This is an issue that copywriters have differing opinions on, even today. According to Hopkins, we should always present the attractive side of a subject, not the offensive side. Rather than focusing on the ills the product is meant to cure, we should focus on the greater health and happiness the reader will experience, thanks to the advertised product.

As we discussed earlier, and as you know from your own experience watching television or reading ads in publications or online, many advertisers today use scare tactics. This is especially true of financial-based pieces addressing current economic conditions or even health-based pieces that talk about illnesses. Sometimes you really do have to paint a clear picture of how bad things are before presenting your product as the solution. Even then, in most cases the headline should

promise that the reader will discover a solution to the problems exposed by the first part of the piece. Once the negatives
of the situation are explained, the piece should concentrate on
how the advertised product will change the reader's life for the
better. Hopkins is right when he says:

> *No toothpaste manufacturer ever made an impression
> by picturing dingy teeth. Or by talking decay and pyor-
> rhea. The successes have been made by featuring the
> attractive sides.*

You can't argue with that. Hopkins tells us that people
are "seeking advantages, improvements, new ways to satisfy
desires." Of course, the best practice is to test everything yourself. Don't assume you know the best way to position your
product. Test to find out what really works.

∎ *Test your headline to find what appeals the most.* Hopkins
always ran keyed tests that compared one headline with another. If you find that one kind of headline appeals to 25 percent
of readers and another one appeals to 50 percent, you must
distribute their use accordingly.

Hopkins said you must understand psychology in creating
headlines (and promotional copy in general). One writer tries
to flatter his readers; another tries to humiliate. One appeals to
readers' self-interest, while another appeals to service. One can
go even further in using psychology to appeal to people's pride
or in making them feel their individuality will be enhanced by
using the product.

To be able to make these appeals, a copywriter needs an
understanding of what makes human beings tick. Hopkins
said this understanding comes from a writer's instincts and
can't really be taught:

> *They come through kindly instinct, through love and
> understanding, through desires to please and serve.
> No man out of tune with his fellows can be taught
> them.*

That puts a big responsibility on writers and promoters, which not everyone can rise to. To be able to appeal to the best in other people, we have to be in touch with the best in ourselves. It says a lot about Hopkins himself, and one would wish that everyone, in any profession, would have such values.

Hopkins concluded that winning ads came not only from superior science and strategy, but also from knowing more and being better grounded and shrewder than one's rivals. As he said:

The only way to that end is to start with fixed principles, proved by decades of experience, from which you never swerve.

We can be very grateful to Claude Hopkins for sharing his discoveries and making it so much easier for promoters of all kinds to create materials that really work.

THE SIX ESSENTIALS—PLUS THAT EXTRA-SPECIAL INGREDIENT

Now we move along to the powerful secrets of writing great copy from another of our legends. There were few copywriters who were as effective at selling a product or an idea as Robert Collier. He knew what it took to get people's attention, to build a desire in them for the product, to induce a sense of urgency, and to get them to take action.

To those of us reading Collier's letters today, their language may seem a bit stilted and old-fashioned—even quaint. We must remember that these letters were appropriate for the audience of the time, and that they sold millions of dollars' worth of goods. These letters saved many companies from financial ruin.

One of Collier's prime points was that it is necessary to lead up to a sale. You must follow a process that involves getting people to take small steps. This starts a momentum that can eventually lead prospects to taking the big step of ordering the product.

Clearly what Collier is talking about is a precursor to what's called "content marketing" today. Online, we can bide our time, giving people a lot of free content, which eventually may lead to a sale. This approach is completely consistent with Collier's thinking. Content marketing would have been difficult and expensive to do back in Collier's day. But now that we can market online, it can be done much more efficiently and cheaply.

In his classic work, *The Robert Collier Letter Book*, Collier laid out his process to create a guide for those who would follow in his footsteps. It's important to realize that for Collier, it was only a guide. He did not try to dictate to other writers how they should illustrate their points or what wording they should use.

One of the things that was so admirable about him was that while he presented rules for copywriters to follow, he understood these were just the basic bones of the piece. They were a starting point that had worked well for him. But ultimately, it was up to the creativity of each writer to flesh out the piece however he or she wanted.

Collier always encouraged new ideas and new approaches. So while he presented what he called the six essentials of any good sales letter, he also said:

These rules, of course, are for the man or woman who is studying the art of writing successful letters. After a time, they come to be almost second nature, so that you weigh each of these features without being conscious that you are doing so.

He added that these rules were only the mechanics of the letter; real letter writing started from these basics.

Let's first look at Collier's list of the six essentials, and then examine that extra-special ingredient he believed was necessary to rise above these mechanical rules and create a truly great sales letter. I want to start by pointing out that these essentials hold for any kind of writing you may be doing. These points are really about building a line of argument that will bring individuals from knowing nothing about you or your product all the way to taking whatever action you desire. This is a process of developing influence over people, whether it's getting them to buy something, vote for you, come back to your next blog post, or just share your message with others.

The Six Essentials

You can think of the following six points as a kind of "Sales Letter Writing 101." These are the six components that Collier believed to be the basis of every great sales letter—although it is not necessary for them to always be presented in this order:

1. *The Opening.* You need to start off with something that will immediately capture and hold your readers' attention. When your readers first view your ad or website, they're probably thinking about something in particular. They're looking for information on a specific topic because they have a problem they need to solve. Or they want to find the perfect gift for someone. Or they're just aimlessly surfing the web, while their background thoughts are about how depressed they are or what that cute guy at work thinks about them.

   They're in an "internal conversation." Somehow you have to jump into your readers' existing train of thought so they are immediately interested in and curious about what you have to tell them.

   A good opening will get through and motivate people to read the rest of what you have to say. Without that, readers may cast the letter aside or click to the next website before you get the chance to present your case.

2. *The Description or Explanation.* Now you have to introduce readers to what you're all about—what product or idea you're trying to sell them. This is where you lay out your basic proposition, presenting the important features and some of the necessary details. You prepare your readers to see things your way by giving them the groundwork of information upon which your arguments will rest.

3. *The Motive or Reason Why.* Here you move past the intellectual and into the emotional. Readers should long for your product, or feel motivated to give to your cause, or desire to do whatever you're trying to influence them to do. You must impel them to take the action you are going to propose.

   This requires that you go beyond merely describing your proposition. You have to get your readers to understand what your product will do for them, or how good they'll feel if they do what you suggest. This is where you lay out all the benefits they will experience if they take the action you want them to.

4. *The Proof or Guarantee.* Even when you make great arguments for your case, people may still be a bit skeptical. They may be concerned that they may do something they might later regret. Now you have to make your readers feel comfortable about their decision to respond to your offer.

   You do that by giving them proof that what you are telling them is true (for example, by backing up your arguments with scientific data or presenting testimonials from other satisfied buyers). You provide some kind of guarantee that they will not lose anything if they take you up on your offer and then are not happy with the product. They can return it for a full refund.

5. *The Snapper or Penalty.* Even if people are completely convinced that what you're telling them is right and that they would benefit from following your suggestions, you still have to get over their basic inertia. Getting people to take action requires an extra boost of energy. If they don't act right away, they could soon forget all about you.

   An old saying tells us to "strike while the iron is hot." You want to get your readers to feel that's what they have to do. This is where you induce a sense of urgency that will encourage readers to respond immediately. Make it clear that if they do not respond right away, they will suffer some kind of loss, whether it be monetary or some kind of prestige or opportunity.

6. *The Close.* By this time, hopefully, you've got your readers eager and ready to take action. In the close, you tell them exactly what they need to do, with complete instructions for how to do it. First, you want a very clear call to action: "Call Now," "Click This Link," "Come to Our Store Before the End of the Month."

Second, you want to make it easy for them to take the final steps to order, request a call by a salesperson, or whatever the goal of the letter is. Make the phone number, website address, email, or link or whatever it is very obvious.

These six essentials should be familiar to you if you've ever read any kind of ad or sales piece, and they certainly make logical sense. It takes more than this, though, to produce something that really works.

That Extra-Special Ingredient Needed for Exceptional Promotional Writing

There is one more ingredient that the letter writer, blogger, or applicant must bring to the task if the result is going to be successful at motivating people to take action. It's really simple. If you want to persuade other people to love something, you have to love it yourself. According to Collier:

It is getting the feel of your message that counts.

If you're completely dry, you can't write a good promotional piece. It won't have any life in it. A good copywriter or promoter gets excited over an idea. That excitement gets conveyed into the writing, and that's what really grabs people.

Excitement is that extra-special ingredient.

Collier told the story of the first sales letter he wrote. At that time, he was working for a coal company located in a small town in West Virginia. He had no training or experience as a copywriter, but he got an idea for what made his company's coal better than their competitors' for a specific use. I won't explain the details to you, but the point is that he became really excited about this idea. As he put it:

I was full of an idea, and it bubbled out all over the letter.
And that is what counts.

His enthusiasm came across in the letter and made it convincing. It certainly convinced the right people, because it led to a huge number of orders for the coal from gas companies.

Enthusiasm like this is the key to selling anything, even a commodity like coal. The ability of a great marketer to take an ordinary commodity and turn it into a specialty item is game-changing. This is being done all the time online today. Marketers start with a commodity, but the way it's sold makes it look so different from the competition—so much more exciting.

You have to find something that really makes your product or service stand out, something you feel compelled to tell people about, something that makes you feel excited. Then you have to make sure the enthusiasm you feel comes across in whatever you write. That's what breathes life into it. And that's the critical lesson from this legendary letter writer I want to get across here. I think this point is essentially the same as what another of our legendary copywriters, David Ogilvy, referred to as "the big idea."

To summarize, there are two critical aspects to creating successful promotions of any kind. First, you have to follow the basics: the six essential elements we listed above. But that's not enough. You must also add that extra-special ingredient: your enthusiasm for your product or service. That's what really motivates people to read what you have to say and then act on your offer.

When you're excited about something, others will be too.

If you're in business, running a political campaign, or promoting anything else, there's something you love about it, something you believe makes you stand out from your competitors. Start with the basics, capture that enthusiasm in everything you create for that promotion, and people will respond.

CHAPTER 5

SECRETS OF WRITING GREAT COPY—PART II

O VER THE YEARS, OUR LEGENDS have amassed a treasure trove of very specific information on how to create effective copy. In Chapter 4, we looked at advice from Hopkins and Collier. In this chapter, we'll look at guidance from Caples and Ogilvy.

HOW TO INCREASE THE SELLING POWER OF ANYTHING YOU WRITE

As you recall, John Caples was the master of direct-response advertising who first became known in 1926 when he launched this now-classic headline:

> They Laughed When I Sat Down at the Piano
> But When I Started to Play!

But Caples was more than a great writer. He was also an advocate of testing every aspect of an advertisement to make sure you, the advertiser, were getting the most bang for your buck.

In his book *Tested Advertising Methods*, he gave specific advice on such issues as how to write headlines that draw the reader's attention and how to use illustrations in ads. What made this advice so powerful is that it was based on years of testing with actual ads. He was not just giving his opinion. He was reporting on his results from the field.

I thought it would be interesting to look at some of Caples' findings when it came to writing effective copy that really sells. He offered a list of 20 methods that he found increased the pulling power of his ads. Most, if not all, of these methods are still relevant to copywriters working today.

Whether you're doing the writing yourself or you have to decide whether the copy of a writer you've hired will get the job done for you, see if you can glean valuable insights from Caples' 20 methods. There are a few I want to emphasize in more detail, so I will address those first.

1. *Use present tense, second person.* When we read any kind of promotional copy, our favorite word is "you." When we see "you," it means the writer is talking directly to us. It encourages us to picture ourselves with the product. There may be times when it's appropriate to use the third person— for example, when talking about "those people" who don't have the finer taste or understanding that "you" do or when explaining the faults of the competition. In general, try to stick to "you" and speak in the present tense as much as possible, not about the past or future.

   Don't say: Buyers will experience vibrant health with a daily dose of aloe vera juice.

   Do say: You experience vibrant health with a daily dose of aloe vera juice.

2. *Use subheads.* Caples found that every page of mail order advertising should have three subheads. I think this may

have been necessary when ads were dense with copy and the use of illustrations was not as sophisticated as modern artists and printing techniques allow for. Today you can get away with fewer subheads if you have a huge headline, color illustrations, and a lot of white space.

The value of subheads—in addition to making the piece more interesting to the eye and breaking up the copy into digestible bits—is that they allow people to get a summary of your pitch even if they don't have the time to read all the copy. An intriguing subhead may also get prospects to dig deeper into copy they might have otherwise skimmed. So use as many subheads as seem right to get your message across.

3. *Use a simple style of writing.* The purpose of your ad is to sell a product or service, not to impress the reader with your brilliant writing. (We've mentioned this idea several times before.) Also, you want your writing to carry the readers along without putting up any roadblocks to their understanding or interest. If your writing is dense, flowery, or filled with complex images the readers can't relate to, you are going to discourage them from moving forward.

4. *Use simple words.* This is similar to the previous point. If your writing is loaded with long, pompous words that most people don't understand, prospects won't keep reading because it seems like too much work. Make it easy for people to read the ad, get the message, and want to follow your call to action.

5. *Give free information.* To get something, you have to give something. To get your readers' attention, you have to give them something to ensure it will be worth their while to read your copy—and one thing you can give them is free information. Tell them something useful right at the beginning. You can even write that part of your letter in editorial style, rather than making it obvious that you're trying to sell them something.

Another method is to promise at the beginning that they will find valuable information later on in the piece, e.g., "Keep reading for the list of ten foods you should always avoid if you suffer from heartburn."

This is especially easy for online marketers, who can offer a downloadable free premium. Caples would have been as happy as a kid in a candy store if he'd had access to today's online marketing techniques.

Advertisers and copywriters in the past used to advise selling the sizzle, not the steak, meaning they pushed the excitement and "aura" of the product rather than give away the "answers" or the "meat." And in fact, advertising used to be all sizzle and no steak.

Brian, who worked closely with Eugene Schwartz at Boardroom Inc., said Schwartz's copy was all sizzle. It was what they called "fascination" copy, or bullet points, usually with exact page numbers where readers could find the answers—if they bought the product.

Over time, however, as longer magalog and bookalog formats evolved, Brian said advertisers began offering more "steak" in their promotions because the longer format lent itself to giving away more free information, leading up to the call to action and the sale. Plus, no reader would stick with 20 to 32 pages of just sizzle. So as copy got longer, magalog authors started giving away more and more real information. For example, they might say there were seven tips for something in the book they were selling. Then they would list five and hold back two.

A highly successful commodity educator and marketer with whom I worked for more than a decade, said he actually gave away how to trade in his bookalog, and rather than making people think they didn't need his course after all, it made them buy even more. One of his mail pieces was 72 pages long. If he'd given sizzle without free information, he never would have held the reader's attention that long.

Online marketers today have also figured out that if they don't give away a lot of free information before getting readers to the point of sale, there's a big chance they'll lose the prospect before getting to the moment of truth.

6. *Make your copy specific.* We are so accustomed to seeing wild advertising claims, especially on the internet, that we don't really believe them anymore. Wild claims were also made back when Caples was writing. To counteract skepticism, he advised saying, "97,482 people have bought one of these appliances" rather than "Nearly 100,000 of these appliances have been sold." The first statement sounds like a fact. The second sounds like copywriting bluster. Simply put, being more precise with exact numbers or "real data," rather than rounding up or being general, will always enhance your copy.

   And don't just say you're better than your competitor. Say your product is 29 percent more effective. Of course, that requires some effort because you must have the research to back it up, but if you can get it, use it.

7. *Write long copy.* You've probably heard that copy can neither be too long nor too short, just too boring. But if it's done intelligently, longer copy does a much better job of selling than shorter copy. The usual objection Caples heard from clients was that no one would want to read long copy. Caples agreed that no one would want to read long, boring copy printed in dense, small type, but if it were laid out attractively, it was always more effective.

   He suggested you could get the best of both worlds by using headlines and subheads to create a smaller, quicker-to-read piece within the longer piece. Then you would appeal to the skimmers while still providing plenty of sales talk to those who were interested and wanted more information. This is especially important when sending emails or setting up web pages. These can be difficult to read if the copy isn't broken up.

8. *Write more copy than you need to fill the space.* Caples suggested writing more copy than you need and then refining it down. Copy gets better when you start long and then cut it. It gets tighter and more to the point. So don't worry about length while you're writing. Just put down all your ideas in as much detail as you want. Then go back and edit, refining as you go, taking out the excess, rephrasing, and getting your points in the most efficient order.

9. *Avoid helping your competitors.* Don't spend a lot of time talking in general terms about how great your type of product is. Talk more specifically about all the great features of your own product.

   Let's say you're selling a home cleaning service. If you spend most of the ad, sales letter, or web copy describing how nice a homeowner's life will be with someone else doing the cleaning, he or she might agree, go surfing online to see who else is offering cleaning services in the area, and end up hiring someone else! Instead, use your copy to focus on the great features of YOUR cleaning service and how you are so much better than anyone else out there.

10. *Make every advertisement a complete sales talk.* Put your complete sales pitch in every promotional piece. Don't assume your prospect has ever read anything else about you or knows anything about the advantages you offer. Don't talk about half the things that make you stand out in one piece and the other half in another promotional piece. For all you know, you will have just this one shot to make this sale or get someone to your blog. Always make the most of it.

11. *Urge the reader to act.* Caples emphasized that every promotional piece should have a clear call to action: Act now! Call today! Order while supplies last! You've spent your entire piece getting your readers' attention and explaining why

they should want your product or join your cause. Now put the bow on the package. Tell them what you want them to do. And if you can add a sense of urgency by telling them it's a limited-time offer, supplies are limited, or these special prices can't last long, all the better. Without a clear call to action, the rest of the piece, as good as it may be, could be a complete waste.

Now, here are the remaining nine points of Caples' top 20 methods for writing copy that sells:

12. *Put captions under illustrations.* Here Caples quoted Ogilvy: "More people read the captions under illustrations than read the body copy, so never use an illustration without putting a caption under it. Your caption should include the brand name and/or the promise."

13. *Selling copy vs. style copy.* Style copy is flowery language and unsubstantiated claims. Selling copy is simple and proves claims. Caples said, "Advertisers who can trace the sales results from their ads use selling copy."

14. *Arouse curiosity.* No explanation needed here.

15. *Use mail order methods in direct mail advertising.* Rules of good advertising, e.g., a strong headline and opening sentence, work for every medium, including online advertising.

16. *Overstatement vs. understatement.* Avoid advertising bluster. Give supported facts and go for believability.

17. *Avoid trick slogans.* Don't use slogans that are obviously untrue. Caples gave the example of a mint manufacturer whose slogan was "On every tongue"—an obvious impossibility. A more effective slogan would be "The flavor lasts."

18. *Get help from others.* Find a sounding board to give you honest opinions on what you write.

19. *Do not say that a salesperson will call.* You will cut down responses to your offer for a free item if you tell prospects

you'll be following up with a call (or letters or emails). Don't tell them your sales plan. Caples said this could reduce responses to coupons by 75 percent.

20. *Study the selling copy in mail order catalogs.* At the time Caples was writing, mail order catalogs had the best copy-writers. He simply meant you should learn how to write great copy by reading the best. Great advice to follow today in your own medium.

Caples' copywriting principles are as useful and relevant today as they were when he used them to run hugely successful campaigns so many years ago.

Now let's examine some of the great secrets offered by the legendary David Ogilvy.

HOW TO PRODUCE ADVERTISING THAT SELLS

In 1983 Ogilvy wrote about his experiences on a number of famous ad campaigns and commented on different aspects of the business in his book *Ogilvy on Advertising*. In Chapter 2 he gave a rather lengthy list of qualities he believed were essential to creating a successful ad campaign. He called it "How to Produce Advertising That Sells." Let's look at just some of the main points made by this master advertising legend, as I think all of them are still on the money today—and they apply to any kind of promotion you may be involved in.

Do Your Homework on Your Product

In order to create advertising that sells, you have to do your research first and then let that guide the way you write about your product. Begin by finding out everything you can about the product itself. What are its features? What are its advantages over its competitors? What are some interesting facts about how it is made or the ingredients that go into it?

Learning all this can help you hit upon the "big idea" around which you will build your ad. It was this kind of research that helped

Ogilvy come up with one of the most famous ad headlines of all time, which we looked at earlier:

At 60 miles an hour the loudest noise in this new Rolls-Royce comes from the electric clock.

As we've already seen, he didn't even write that headline himself. It was an actual line from a company report that his research turned up and his instincts recognized as a "big idea."

Do Your Homework on Your Competitors

Ogilvy thought this would give you your bearings. If you research your competitors, you know what kind of advertising statements and methods are standard in your niche. This knowledge enables you to adapt some ideas that you like for yourself as well as to recognize a different, more revolutionary approach that you could take to stand out.

Survey Consumers of the Product

Learn how they think about it. Find out what language they use when talking about the product, what aspects of the product matter most to them, and what kind of promise you could make about the product that would appeal to them.

You shouldn't guess at any of these things. You can get the facts through surveying prospects and doing your homework on the product and your competitors. Once you have the facts, you can craft a piece designed to appeal to your best prospects.

Positioning

Ogilvy had the best definition of what he called this curious verb:

What the product does, and who it is for.

Positioning is about deciding who your audience is, whom your ad should appeal to, and what advantages you need to stress about your product so it will appeal to your target audience. The example Ogilvy gave is the approach he took to advertising a product that was just coming out called Dove soap. He could have positioned it as the perfect cleanser for men's dirty hands. The better positioning, which he used, was as a moisturizing soap for women with dry skin. This approach turned out to be highly successful and is still the basis of the company's ads today.

So how can you know how to position your product?

Consider who your best prospect is and gear your ads to that person. Don't try to please everyone. You can't. A dress shop might position itself as the trendy place where teenagers and young women in their twenties shop, or a sophisticated store for upwardly mobile professionals, or the place where mature matrons of a certain income level buy clothing for special occasions and cruises. You will never appeal to all these audiences, so you must choose which one will work best for you. Then your advertising should be positioned to reflect the kind of business you are and the type of customer you want to attract.

Similarly, if you are writing a blog for young muscle builders, you want to use keywords in your pieces that will be picked up in online searches by your best prospects. You would use different language to attract middle-aged men who want to exercise to improve their health. Know your audience and position yourself accordingly.

Always write in the language and terminology of your core audience. Your concern shouldn't be whether your copy may be too sophisticated or simplistic; it should be whether you're using the right language for the right audience.

Choose the Right Brand Image

When you think of brand image, a number of famous examples come to mind. You may think of classic advertising figures, such as the Marlboro Man, the Schweppes Man, Orville Redenbacher, Colonel Sanders, Queen Latifah selling Covergirl, or Andie MacDowell in ads for L'Oréal. The idea is to have some recognizable image associated with your product that supports its positioning. It's often a person, but it can also just be the product itself, like Coca-Cola, which is a brand image recognized around the world.

Many marketers associate their product with a person who seems to be writing the sales letter or the web copy. Institutions do this too. The Mayo Clinic makes heavy use of its image and reputation to sell publications and supplements.

Could you or someone else at your company represent and speak for your products and services? It needs to be an appealing and/or authoritative figure. You could set this person up as the recognizable face of your company. Done correctly, it could increase brand loyalty and boost your business.

Brian implements what he calls the "bloodhound approach" or "watchdog approach." In this case, the face of the company is not a practitioner or an institution, but someone who is watching out for the consumer. This can be great positioning. For example, Boardroom Inc. presented Marty Edelston as the "bloodhound" who was going to take care of consumers and protect their health and money from people who would try to destroy it or steal it from them. He was not an expert himself, but a watchdog for others.

An example of a headline they used was "Twelve Smiling Swindlers." Underneath was a list of people we encounter every day, such as a lawyer, accountant, and car salesman. Marty was protecting everybody from these "swindlers." Brian told me he recommends his clients consider whether they can use the bloodhound approach to build a brand image.

What's the Big Idea?

Sometimes, through genius or just plain luck—often based on tons of research that laid the groundwork for the "aha" moment—someone comes up with a big idea. Ogilvy's Rolls-Royce ad was a prime example. So was representing Pepperidge Farm baked goods with an old-fashioned bakery wagon pulled by horses. Another great inspiration was the Jack-in-the-Box clown as a business executive in a suit. These are all brilliant ideas that have worked for decades to sell products.

One colleague of mine always wore a cowboy hat in his promotions, and he put pictures of cowboy hats on all his literature. He was not a cowboy and was not raised on a ranch, but that hat was a perfect and highly recognizable representation of his maverick style. Maybe you can come up with something like that to represent what you do. Ideas like this don't come along every day, but if you ever get one, keep using it.

Identify the "Positively Good"

It would be great if you could prove that your product was significantly better than anything your rivals can provide, but that's not always possible. Sometimes you and your competitors offer an equivalent product or service. But that shouldn't be a barrier to making you stand out in your advertising. You don't have to convince customers that nobody else on the planet can rival you. You just have to convince them that your product is "positively good." If they believe you're good, and they're not so sure about your competitors, they'll give you the business.

All you have to do is focus on telling prospects how good you are. List in detail all your great qualities. Create confidence in the value of your product. You don't have to compare yourself or mention your competition at all. And keeping in mind some of the advice we heard earlier, don't boast or brag with empty statements. Use facts and descriptions to confidently put the spotlight on what you provide.

Repeat Your Winners

If your promotional efforts are working well, keep repeating them until they stop working. There's no need to keep reinventing the wheel. And don't change just for the sake of change. At the same time, you don't want to be caught short if what you've been doing suddenly stops working. To avoid being caught in a bind like that, you should always be testing alternatives. For example, if you're doing direct mail, as long as your control piece (your basic advertising piece against which you test any variations you come up with) is out-pulling anything else you've tried, keep using it. When a new piece out-pulls the old one, roll out to a bigger campaign with the new one. This is just as true online, although on the internet it can happen in minutes, rather than months.

In determining which piece is your winner, you must know whether the data you're looking at is accurate—bad data is worse than no data. Making this call is based on statistical significance, which is too complicated to go into here, but simply put, you need to truly know you have a new winner before you get rid of the old one. Yes, we have to make decisions faster now than we did before, but that is no excuse not to be disciplined about your data. More than ever, we must have data we can rely on.

Strive for Word-of-Mouth

Ogilvy said that sometimes advertising campaigns go beyond themselves and enter the culture. People go around humming jingles or repeating ad slogans. Sometimes they'll be parodied on *Saturday Night Live*! This is great free publicity. The opportunity for word-of-mouth advertising is even greater today, with the growing importance of social media and the potential for friends to share information about you with hundreds or even thousands of people.

You never know when something will take off like this. Ogilvy called it "manna from heaven." You can't create this kind of buzz, but you can encourage it by suggesting your customers share information about you with their friends. And if it ever happens that you do find yourself "going viral," stay on top of it and take advantage of your golden moment. It may not last long, but it can put you or your business on the map.

It's great to be in a position to ride the wave of a success you didn't predict. For example, Pabst Blue Ribbon, which is a classic old beer, never advertised to a youthful market. Recently they realized that young people were spreading the word that it's a cool beer to drink. The youth market has become quite substantial for them, all through word-of-mouth.

As a second example, *Brides* magazine, which usually retains subscribers for about a year as young women prepare for their wedding, came to realize many years ago that the magazine is being bought on newsstands by young, inner-city women who are not preparing for a wedding, but using the magazine as a dream book for inspiration. The magazine doesn't actively market to them, but they know that audience is significant. So they added a few articles and features to support that interest. Again, the surge in readership was not the result of advertising, but word-of-mouth.

MORE DAVID OGILVY SECRETS: NECESSARY EXPENSES, SECRET WEAPONS, AND KILLER COPY

Ogilvy was a master at developing techniques for persuasively presenting information on behalf of his clients that turned readers into buyers. In one of his books, Ogilvy addressed the question of why a business should advertise at all.

Advertising can be very expensive. Advertisers know they have to keep their name before the public, and they fear their competition will get the jump on them if they don't. At the same time, they may secretly wonder whether their ads are worth the cost. Do they actually influence people to buy the product? Unless advertisers do the proper research, they may not know if ads increase their profits at all.

Ogilvy cites the story of a man who asked Mr. Wrigley (of Wrigley gum) why he spent so much on advertising when he already had captured the lion's share of the market. Wrigley asked the man how fast he thought the train they were riding on was going. The man estimated about 90 miles per hour. "Well," Wrigley said, "do you suggest we unhitch the engine?" Ogilvy's point in retelling this story (that is still viable today) is you have to keep your momentum going. Even a successful business has to stay ahead of the competition, and advertising is the cheapest form of selling, compared to sending an army of salespeople into people's homes.

Whether you're building a business or keeping it on top, don't begrudge your advertising budget. It's a necessary expense, but it should be spent carefully, and that requires some specialized skills. This goes back to the notion of riding—and then beating—your winning control piece. Brian often says, "The control is your enemy." The day you get a winning promotion—no matter what the medium, online or off—is the day you start trying to beat it.

Ogilvy's Secret Weapon—Direct Mail!

David Ogilvy was especially known for his brilliant print advertising in magazines and newspapers, but he also saw many advantages in direct mail. In fact, you might say he was a direct marketer in a general advertiser's body.

Yes, Ogilvy was a giant in general advertising. His true genius is that he was one of the first general advertisers who realized the importance of measuring response rates. He was obsessed with accountability and measurability in all advertising—as were all the legends—and direct mail was the medium where they began to perfect this obsession.

Ogilvy's initial foray into direct mail came when he was an office boy at a London advertising agency. A man came in wanting to advertise a country house he was converting into a hotel. He had just $500 to spend on an ad campaign, and the agency head quickly turned the assignment over to one of his lowliest employees.

The clever young man (Ogilvy) invested the small budget into penny postcards (covered, no doubt, in his own glowing copy) and mailed them to wealthy people who lived in the area. Six weeks later, when the hotel opened, it had a full house. As Ogilvy said of his success:

I had tasted blood.

After that he called direct mail his "first love and secret weapon." His use of the medium led to "the avalanche of new business acquisitions that made Ogilvy & Mather an instant success."

For many years the direct mail industry lagged, but it saw a burst of new growth with the coming of computers. Ogilvy valued modern computers for enabling advertisers to select highly targeted names from mailing lists based on factors such as demographics and buying habits. They allowed advertisers to merge and purge lists to remove duplications and the names of people who had requested not to receive mailings. They allowed personalization of letters by printing the recipient's name multiple times within a mailing.

Ogilvy lauded direct mail for allowing advertisers to measure the results of their mailings and perform tests of different variables, leading to more and more successful campaigns. According to Ogilvy:

In direct mail, testing is the name of the game.

Next to positioning a product, Ogilvy said the most important variables to test are price, terms of payment, the use of premiums (primarily referred to today as bonuses), and the format of a mailing (e.g., postcard vs. letter, letter vs. magalog, etc.).

Sometimes testing like this leads to unexpected results. For example, Ogilvy once ran a direct mail campaign to sell collections of silver, gold, and platinum coins from the Moscow Olympic Games. He found that a letter selling only the silver coins resulted in more sales of complete collections than did a letter that tried to sell the complete collection in the first place. There's no telling why that was the case, but the lesson is clear: testing is critical to discovering how to make the most lucrative sales.

Another of his findings was that fewer people will respond to an offer asking for the full price of an item in cash, but the customers who do respond have greater lifetime value (that is, they spend more money over a long period of time), leading to more profitable mailings. Ogilvy said:

Only testing will tell. The more you test, the more profitable your direct mail will become.

He suggested turning successful pieces into "control" pieces, against which variable test pieces could be compared. In this way you would know exactly what you were doing as you made changes to get better and better results. Innovations could boost results, but you wouldn't know unless you ran the appropriate statistical tests.

Today, direct mail doesn't always get the respect it deserves. Online marketers often see "snail mail" as passé. Brian likes to joke with online marketers: "Have you heard of that NEW medium called direct mail?" As we stated earlier in our discussion of cross-channel marketing, direct mail could be an important element in your mix, even if you currently have no experience in it. The fact is, in today's marketing landscape, direct mail has become a secret weapon for many online companies.

You might consider rereading this section about Ogilvy on direct mail, and look at it in the context of your own online business, especially with regard to multichannel marketing and Brian's concept of "O . . . to O . . . to O" that we looked at earlier in Chapter 4.

Tips for Writing Copy That Sells

Now let's get to Ogilvy's suggestions for how to write more effectively and get a bigger response. Whether he was writing copy for direct mail or print advertising, Ogilvy had some tricks up his sleeve that worked well for influencing people to buy the product he was selling. These same techniques can work for any kind of promotional writing today, offline or online.

Readers Read Ads as Individuals, Usually While They Are by Themselves

So don't address them as though they were a crowd in a stadium. It makes you seem cold and distant, when your aim is to be seen as a trusted friend. It also makes the reader's attention flag. As you write your copy, think about the one person you are "talking" to. Pretend you are in a one-on-one conversation with that single reader, presenting information on what you are offering, "one human being to another, and second person singular."

You Can't Bore People into Doing What You Want Them to Do

You can only interest them into doing it. So hold their interest by writing short sentences arranged in brief paragraphs. Don't use difficult words. If you're not sure whether a word is too difficult for the average person, Ogilvy suggested you take a bus trip to Iowa, talk to a farmer for a week, then come back by train and talk to your fellow passengers. And then, at the end of that time, see if you still want to use that word. There may be something dated in the way Ogilvy described this fact-finding adventure, but the advice is still valuable today. Listen to the people you want to appeal to, and then address them in language they understand and can relate to.

Don't Write Essays
That means don't wax philosophic or get too theoretical. Your copy should tell your readers exactly what your product or service will do for them and how it will improve their lives. Make sure your copy is filled with specifics that make it easy for readers to picture how they will personally benefit from using what you are offering them.

It Is Always a Great Advantage to Be Able to
Write Copy in the Form of a Story
An example Ogilvy gave was the hugely popular ad for Zippo lighters that used the headline:

> The Amazing Story of a Zippo That Worked After
> Being Taken from the Belly of a Fish

And of course there is that classic John Caples ad with the headline:

> They Laughed When I Sat Down at the Piano
> But When I Started to Play!

Not only do stories like these grab your prospects' interest, but people also remember stories, which can carry the influence of the ad (or the website copy or the blog) beyond the initial reading. Just make sure there's a strong connection between the story and the product so that remembering the story automatically brings up an image of the product.

Avoid Using Analogies and Superlatives
People often misunderstand analogies, especially if you don't have their undivided attention. For example, if you show a picture of a Rembrandt and say, "Just as a Rembrandt portrait is a masterpiece, so too is our product," many readers will think you're selling

Rembrandt prints. If they're not interested in buying a Rembrandt, they may not even read the rest of the piece. And superlatives ("We're simply the best in the world!") convince nobody, which is the same advice we've heard now from several of our legends.

If You Have Testimonials from Happy Customers, Be Sure to Include Them

Many great ads are built around a heartfelt testimonial, but be careful because testimonials from celebrities have been known to backfire. People will often remember the celebrity but forget the product. If you get a great testimonial from someone similar to your target audience, it can do a good job of strengthening your sales pitch.

It Is Often Wise to Include the Price of Your Product in an Advertisement

People generally have good recall of the price, and they like to know what to expect. This may work especially well for things like cars and refrigerators, where people already have a fairly good idea of the cost of these items. I have found, however, that for some items, like expensive coaching sessions, where the need is not that obvious and the value can't be pinned down to anything specific, having the reader call for more information is often a better way to go. That way a trained salesperson can soften the blow and more fully explain why the item in question is so valuable.

In General, Longer Copy Is More Effective Than Shorter Copy

Split-run tests invariably find that longer copy outsells shorter copy. But again, you must make sure the copy is interesting or no one will read it.

Ogilvy was a master copywriter with many successful campaigns, so if you're looking to judge the quality of the marketing information you're about to send out, be sure to look at it from the perspective of his advice. Ultimately, however, the final determination of the quality of your copy is how well it sells your product to your target audience—knowing that requires research and testing.

FINAL THOUGHTS ON WRITING GREAT COPY

We've now looked at four of our legends' rules for writing great copy. As you read through them, it becomes clear that they offer similar advice:

- Speak to a single reader, not a crowd.
- Keep your language and images simple.
- Find out everything you can about your product and write specific copy that comes out of that information.
- Avoid empty boasts.
- Back everything up with facts.
- Longer copy outsells shorter copy, as long as it holds the reader's interest.
- Strong openings and clear calls to action are mandatory.

It's also clear that the advice offered by our legends is universal despite being written decades ago. These rules work for any medium, even though they were laid down long ago by men you may have never heard of before picking up this book.

CHAPTER 6

HEADLINES: IT'S ALL ABOUT GETTING YOUR PROSPECT'S ATTENTION

I F YOU HAVE SOMETHING IMPORTANT you want to say to someone, the first thing you have to do is get that person's attention. Otherwise you're just talking to yourself. When you're trying to get the attention of people nearby, you do it by calling out to them—your voice cuts through the surrounding noise and gets them to focus on you. But when you're communicating through a written sales piece, an email, or the copy on a web page, you have to "call out" to your audience in a different way.

The way to get people's attention in those situations is through your headline—the bold words at the top of the page that people see at a glance. Depending on whether what they see interests them, they'll either go on to read the rest or move on to something else.

Our legends understood how important it was for a piece to have a strong, enticing headline, and they have a great deal to share with us on how to create headlines that do their job. You can use their secrets to make every message you send out more effective.

BE SHREWDER THAN YOUR RIVALS

Let's start with Claude Hopkins, who reported he had seen an eight- to ten-times increase in an ad's results just by making a small adjustment to a headline. He stressed that headlines have the purpose of "saluting" your target audience, and he likened it to a hotel bellboy calling for Mr. Jones or Mr. Smith: "We have a message for you."

Most people today have no idea what it means for a bellboy to be calling out a patron's name in a hotel lobby, but it happened quite frequently before the era of cellphones and instant messaging. The bellboy marched through the hotel ringing a bell and shouting the name of a patron to give him a message that he had a visitor, a phone call, or a telegram.

Just as our legends emphasized headlines, online marketers today must put their attention on creating great subject lines. In talking with Brian about subject lines in today's very competitive (and very noisy) email marketing world, he says he has seen open rates increase five to ten times, just by changing a subject line. It can't be overemphasized how important choosing the right subject line is in your email marketing efforts.

If people decide what deserves their attention based on the headline (or subject line), the promoter must determine what headline will have the greatest appeal to the target audience. The only way to know that for sure is to run a series of tests. Hopkins said that to do anything less would be a "tremendous waste."

It takes scientific study for promoters to establish what approach will work best for their target audience: flattery, fear, self-interest? Hopkins suggested one of the best ways to determine this is to canvass the target audience—even if it means making personal contact with them, perhaps by calling some people or sending them a survey. This takes effort and an initial outlay of money, but he insisted it's well worth it in the long run:

The man who wins out and survives does so only because of superior science and strategy. He must know more, must be better grounded, must be shrewder than his rivals.

Regardless of what you're promoting, you would do well to learn as much as you can about your target audience and how to get their attention. What words appeal to them? What problems do they have that, if you refer to them, will make them sit up and take notice? You may have to send out a survey, or perhaps you can just talk to some of them. You'll find it's worth whatever effort you put into getting this information.

UNDERSTAND THE REAL PURPOSE OF YOUR HEADLINE

Next I want to look at what Eugene Schwartz had to say about headlines, because it gives us an interesting perspective on what a good headline is all about. Schwartz told us that, in spite of what many of us may believe, "the headline does not sell." That's not its purpose. Its purpose is to capture attention.

As people read through their mail, you have only ten seconds to catch their interest. During those ten seconds, people decide to either keep reading the piece or throw it away. The headline's only purpose is to get people to read the rest of the piece. It doesn't sell a product, confirm a point of view, argue for or against any position, or say anything about the advertiser. It just has to get people to read the next paragraph.

Schwartz was talking about direct-mail sales pieces. Think about how much less time it takes for someone to make a decision while surfing the web or going through dozens of emails in a crowded inbox. Brian always tells me he pictures a direct mail prospect sorting their mail over the wastebasket, and he disagrees that we even have ten seconds to capture their attention. In fact, he says we have just "1.8 seconds" to capture a prospect's attention. If the prospect is reading an email promotion with one hand on a mouse, it's probably "0.6 seconds." So in Brian's opinion, the engagement level with direct mail is three times longer than it is with an email.

If you can only count on about one-third the attention span with email, it's more important than ever to have a headline or subject line that grabs attention and entices the prospect to read on. How long should the headline be? There's no universal length that will be right for every piece. The headline just has to be long enough to stop prospects from throwing the piece away and get them to read the next paragraph. As Schwartz told us:

> *The headline sells the first line. The first line sells the second line. The second line sells the third line. And the third line sells the fourth line, etc.*

You just want the reader to keep moving through your copy. Remember, your readers may not be ready to accept certain ideas until they've been prepared for it. You can say things in the middle of a piece that readers would never believe in a headline. As Schwartz said:

> *If he is prepared to believe, he is prepared to buy.*

Your job as a marketer is to build your argument so you make the right points at the right time. If you're not using your headline to sell, what do you want to put in the headline? First, you want to include some kind of promise, and it's especially strong if it's connected to intrigue—something people find personally fascinating, with a bit of mystery attached. Second, the mechanism of the headline is to capture an emotion. If readers are intrigued and their emotions are touched, they will keep reading.

How do you find your headline? The product itself gives it to you. You should be working from copious notes based on interviews or going through the manuscript of the book you're trying to sell. Of course, if you're selling yourself and your personal blog, or explaining why you're the best job candidate, you could make a list of everything special you have to offer and get your headline from there.

Go through your notes again and again until a picture begins to emerge of the problem the product addresses, how it resolves that problem, and who your audience is. Schwartz used this method to come up with the following headline that sold huge numbers of books:

Sneaky Little Arthritis Tricks, Natural Foods and
Do-It-Yourself Secrets That Pain-Proofed Over 100
Men and Women Like You.

By the way, Brian wants to point out that anyone who spends even 15 minutes a day on the internet has probably seen an ad promising "sneaky little tricks." Now it should be clear that an internet marketer didn't invent that line. More important, keep in mind that the "eternal truths" in headline writing we are reading about today have been used for decades—even centuries. There's so much for us to learn by uncovering these gems from the past. So study Schwartz's headline closely, and all its brilliance will reveal itself to you.

- It makes it clear who should be interested in reading more (anyone in pain, especially people with arthritis).
- It promises a simple, inexpensive solution (using natural foods and do-it-yourself methods).
- It implies that these "secrets" are not broadly known and that the reader will be let in on something special.
- And it promises that these secrets have successfully helped others just "like you."

For people suffering from the pain of arthritis who may have tried everything they could get their hands on to no avail, this would certainly seem like something worth looking into further by reading the rest of the sales piece. If you follow up a headline like this with a dynamite first paragraph that strengthens the points in the headline and ends with a hook to the second paragraph, you're well on your way to bringing in your prospect.

Here are some ways to create a dynamite headline that Brian learned from Eugene Schwartz and Marty Edelston.

Rewrite a Cliché for Your Purpose

Brian reminded me that what looks like a cliché in a headline can be super effective because it uses language your prospect is used to hearing.

For example, a cliché often used at Boardroom Inc. was "What your mother never told you." They adapted this to "What your lawyer never told you," "What your doctor never told you," "What your accountant never told you," etc.

Add an Element of Tension

This happens when parts of a headline look like they contradict each other. Brian gave me an example of adding tension to a headline they used at Boardroom Inc. for an estate-planning book:

> What your lawyer never told you when you
> made out your will.

You can find hundreds of examples of powerful headlines like this in the "swipe files" of great copywriters—and from the experiences of industry insiders like Brian.

Remember the "Twelve Smiling Swindlers" we mentioned when we talked about the bloodhound approach in Chapter 5? That was the cover headline of a 20-plus-page promotion (called a "magalog") for a book that sold hundreds of thousands of copies. It was one of the most powerful headlines Brian used at Boardroom Inc. because of the tension it raised. The urgency to find out which of the smiling swindlers was ripping them off really got prospects to read on.

Raise Questions People Want Answers To

Brian gave examples of "fascinations" (i.e., bullet points with accompanying page numbers where buyers will find the answers in the book) from some of his most successful direct marketing packages. Some of these were:

How to know when a slot machine is about to pay off

How to outwit a mugger in a self-service elevator

What never to eat on an airplane

These are all what Brian would call "tension headlines." While these are all examples from his experience at Boardroom Inc., they were written by world-class copywriters who studied with people like Eugene Schwartz and Gary Halbert.

Now, in addition to your main headline, you will probably have several lesser headlines and subheads strewn throughout your piece, especially if it's a long letter, webpage, or email. Each of these subheads should follow the rules of the main headline, carrying forward the logic of your argument and tying one section of the piece to the next. How many should you have? There is no firm rule. You need to put in as many as you need to make the piece work. As the piece develops, this will become clearer.

These principles work for many different kinds of products and methods of selling them. For example, pretend you are a job applicant. You want your resume to stand out from the crowd. Think of the opening lines on your cover letter as a kind of headline, in which you stress how you are unique and what great benefits you can bring to a company. This opening line doesn't have to tell the whole story of who you are. It couldn't possibly. It just has to make you memorable and get the people reading it to go on to the next paragraph of the letter, and then turn to the resume, where you back up everything you promised in your "headline." Look at everything you write in these terms, and you will increase the "selling power" of every job application, self-description on a dating site, or anything else.

OGILVY WISDOM ON HEADLINES

Now let's move on to Ogilvy, who also reported on his research with headlines. He found that advertisements with headlines that promise a benefit are read by four times more people than advertisements without such a headline. As you will recall, his headline for Rolls-Royce is said to be the most famous ever written, so when it comes to headlines, we know anything Ogilvy tells us will be of value.

Surprisingly, he once wrote that much of what he knew about writing effective headlines he learned by studying the way *Reader's Digest* writes its "ingenious" article titles. These titles pique the curiosity of readers and, at the same time, promise all the questions they raise will be answered. As an example, he provided this title that he especially liked:

> What Truckers Say About Your Driving
> Professional drivers sound off on the most common—
> and dangerous—faults of the amateur

This title first gets us curious. We all want to be seen as excellent drivers. It's a point of pride. Now that you mention it, we actually would like to know what truckers think of us.

Then the subhead promises that not only will we learn what professional drivers judge about amateurs like us, but they will also reveal what we do that's dangerous. By reading this article, we'll be safer on the road. Ogilvy said no one could resist reading an article with a title like that.

Ogilvy, whose livelihood depended on getting people to read the ads he wrote for his high-paying clients, found that if he could write headlines that grabbed attention and compelled people to read the rest of the copy, the battle was more than half won. And again, he honed his skill by studying *Reader's Digest* headlines.

This is a great tip for us today. You can find *Reader's Digest*, O magazine, *People* magazine, and other popular publications in grocery stores everywhere. You may already subscribe to some of them, or you can read them for free at your local library. Use them as your own personal mentor for how to write headlines that work.

According to Ogilvy's findings, five times as many readers will look at your headline as will read the rest of your ad. Therefore, "unless your headline sells your product, you have wasted 90 percent of your money." This may seem on the surface to contradict what Schwartz told us earlier, which was that we should not try to sell the product in the headline. I'd like to hear the two discuss the issue, but I don't think their opinions are really that far apart. The Schwartz headline about arthritis secrets does sell the product; it just does it with some subtlety. All Ogilvy is saying is that headlines have to carry important information, which I think Schwartz would agree with. Still, this may be one area where two legends disagree, which means research is the only way to get the answer that works for you.

Continuing with what Ogilvy had to tell us, he said intriguing headlines are good, but only if they also sell the product. On this note, he said it's important to use the product name in the headline. If you don't, the 80 percent of readers who read only the headline and never go on to read the copy will have no idea what the ad is about—again, a complete waste of the advertiser's money.

There are certain elements you can introduce into a headline that add to its power. News about a product is especially effective at getting attention. News can take several forms. Your headline may promise information about a new product that's just come on the market, or it may tell of improvements to familiar products or new ways to use them.

Ogilvy reported that compared to headlines without news, headlines with that newsy element were remembered by 22 percent more readers. And he advised that there's nothing wrong with calling attention to news by using words that may seem a bit trite, but are quite effective—words like amazing, introducing, now, and suddenly. These words work at getting attention and that's all that matters.

Another element of headlines that Ogilvy found attracted more readership was the promise of helpful information. "How to" headlines are especially effective. If your ad is targeting a particular audience, like mothers or skateboarders or physical fitness buffs, call that out in the headline. (Remember, that's what Schwartz did with arthritis sufferers.) It may keep other people from reading the ad, but it's more important to get the attention of the specific people you want, like the bellboy calling out their name in the hotel lobby.

There is conflicting research on how many words a headline should contain. So Ogilvy suggested making your headline as long as it needs to be to convey a message, but short headlines could work well, too. He cited the famous 1960s ad for Volkswagen that had a big picture of the old Beetle, and below it in huge letters the word "Lemon." In many ways this brilliant headline breaks just about every rule that Ogilvy gave us, but you can't argue with success. This award-winning ad gave the Volkswagen company a huge boost.

The "lemon" headline worked because it was both a visual pun and a surprising joke. The visual pun was that the Beetle is shaped like a lemon. The surprise is that the word "lemon" is usually used to refer to a bad car, but in this case, it's used as an endearing description that points out a benefit of the car—its small, cute shape. The ad further played on the "lemon" idea by pointing out a small blemish in the chrome stripping on the glove compartment that had been missed—but was finally caught by the eagle eyes of their scrupulous inspector. The self-deprecating way in which the company used such a tiny defect to call the car a lemon implied the opposite—that the car was tremendously reliable. This ad created tremendous buzz when it came out, and shows that a clever one-word headline can be very successful.

Testing your ads is critical. Feel free to experiment and try something new—that's what the legends did. But always test to see whether it works.

Here are some more bits of Ogilvy's headline wisdom:

▮ *Specific information in headlines is more persuasive than generalities.* So give actual percentages or other figures when you can (e.g., not "Our Washers Get Clothes Cleaner" but "Our Washers Get Clothes 56% Cleaner").

▮ *Headlines in quotation marks increase recall by 28 percent.* Perhaps it draws attention, or makes the headline seem authoritative.

▮ *If you're advertising in a local area, put the name of the city in your headline.* When people see they will be getting information on something local that could concern them, it gets their attention.

Readers skim quickly through magazines, newspapers, and today, across web pages. You want the meaning of your headlines to be grasped immediately. Ogilvy found that in general, clever headlines with tricks, puns, obscure references, and so on were actually counterproductive (notwithstanding the Beetle ad, which is in a class by itself). If people don't get the message immediately, they move on. If the headline looks puzzling, readers just won't want to put in the effort to understand the rest of the piece. Ogilvy made his position very clear: "Your headline should telegraph what you want to say." If you think running an ad without any headline (what Ogilvy called "a headless wonder") might be interesting to try, remember that Ogilvy thought it was "the silliest thing of all."

Ogilvy advised that those who wanted to learn more about writing great headlines should look into John Caples' book *Tested Advertising Methods*, and that's exactly what we will do next. The fact that the legends studied and influenced each other was one of my motivations to write this book.

CAPLES: THE MOST IMPORTANT PART OF AN ADVERTISEMENT

As we've heard from our other legends, Caples found that the most important part of an advertisement was the headline. As an example, he tested the two headlines below, written by the great copywriter Max Sackheim. The two headlines were placed on essentially the same ad. One was a great success. In fact, it is often considered one of the greatest headlines in advertising history. The other one was a failure. Can you guess which was which?

> Headline 1: "Are You Afraid of Making Mistakes in English?"
>
> Headline 2: "Do You Make These Mistakes in English?"

The second headline pulled many more orders and inquiries, and the reason was the use of the word "these." "These" promised that a helpful list of common blunders was included in the ad copy.

This appealed to readers because they would be getting valuable information for free. It also aroused their curiosity and self-interest. No one wants to make embarrassing mistakes, and for those people who pride themselves on their superior language skills, it promised they would get a good laugh by seeing the errors of others. In any case, the headline made them want to read further, which allowed the sales piece to do its job of selling.

Brian recently shared an amazing story with me about the top online marketer in Brazil. This man told Brian he created a subject line that said:

Do you make these mistakes in internet marketing?

He said this was one of the most effective subject lines he ever used, and this is someone who tests subject lines every day in everything he does. John Caples would have been proud, and he didn't even have to do the translation into Portuguese!

The takeaway here is that without a good headline, you can have the best copy in the world, but chances are no one will read it. As a result, the entire ad is a waste.

Caples' Rules for Writing Headlines That Work

After years of testing ad headlines to determine which formula worked best, Caples came up with the following elements of effective headlines. He felt you should always appeal to the reader's:

Self-Interest

This is the first and foremost task of the marketer. Give the reader a reason to look through the rest of the piece, open the email, or click through to the website. This should seem obvious, but this rule is violated again and again.

Interest in News

If you have something new to report—a new product or a change in an old product—make sure to put that fact in the headline. Any news should really be played up in the headline.

Curiosity

Do not merely try to provoke curiosity in a headline. Curiosity can be powerful, but only if it's combined with self-interest and/or news. A headline that is merely clever may please the copywriter, but it will not capture readers.

Positivity

Wherever possible, avoid headlines that only present a gloomy or negative picture. If you need to lead with something negative, always add a positive angle.

Need for Quick and Easy Solutions

Headlines that suggest there is a quick and easy way for readers to get what they want can be very appealing.

Desire for Believability

The headline must be believable. Caples gives the example of a headline that was tested by a correspondence school:

To Men and Women Who Want to
Work Less and Earn More

The ad was a bust because it seemed too good to be true. He offered another example where a headline promising someone could make $9,000 actually pulled better than one promising someone could make $100,000. People at the time couldn't imagine making $100,000. The idea seemed ridiculous and the ad looked like an exaggerated sales pitch, but $9,000 seemed reasonable and attractive enough to get people to respond.

Caples' Rules Work Today

Times change, but people don't. I'm sure you'll find that all of Caples' rules can create great headlines for the types of products we sell today. At their core, landing pages and other online ads that perform extremely well speak directly to real people with real problems in search of real solutions.

And people are people. This means that the rock-bottom, non-negotiable, absolutely essential elements to every "order page," online or offline, are the same. The internet didn't invent them.

And you don't need to either.

The most important point is his overall rule: Test everything. Don't take anyone's word or opinion on any aspect of your marketing. If you want marketing materials that you know work for you, become a scientific advertiser. That's the legendary lesson to take to heart.

WRITING HEADLINES THAT REALLY WORK

Now we turn to the ideas of Gary Halbert. Halbert said writing is not easy (although he offered some great advice for writing without writer's block, which we'll look at in Chapter 7). Writing is especially difficult if you're trying to get people to buy something. Halbert said you had to just start, following something you may have heard of— the AIDA formula. This formula tells us that writing that sells must do four things. You have to:

▌ Get **Attention**
▌ Capture **Interest**
▌ Arouse **Desire** (for what you're selling)
▌ Motivate people to take **Action**

The first step is to capture attention, and the way you do that is by creating what Halbert called a "killer" headline. Here again, Halbert's rules will have a familiar ring. When we see the legends using the same principles, it's a good sign we should be using them as well.

Halbert's Rules for Writing Killer Headlines

Just as our other legends did, Halbert stressed that the headline was crucial to how well a piece would do at getting prospects to take action. He cited some experts who claimed the headline accounted for 80 percent of an ad's success. In his own experience, he found that by writing a new headline for an ad, he could increase its pulling power by 475 percent. For this reason, he put more creative effort into writing headlines than any other aspect of his copywriting. So you can be sure that any advice Halbert gave on how to write headlines will be very instructive. Here are some of his basics:

Rule 1: Call Them by Name!

Nothing captures our attention like hearing our own name. Research shows that if someone across a noisy room says your name, you'll hear it above the din. And thanks to today's printing technology, you can create the same effect in a sales piece. You can even print each prospect's name in the headline of your piece. According to Halbert, using someone's name in the headline is an irresistible draw and "the ultimate way to get attention in a sales letter."

Technology advances in online marketing allow us to take Halbert's rule and apply it in a big way—everywhere. For example, using a personalized URL, or PURL, in the headline of a piece invites readers to visit their own personal website. It's not always possible to do this, though. Fortunately, Halbert offers other techniques you can use to add power to your headlines.

Rule 2: Put News in Your Headline

You want to make readers believe that reading your sales piece will fill them in on important happenings. Maybe they will learn about a new scientific discovery or secret technique a celebrity uses to be beautiful or successful. If prospects invest a little of their time to read the piece, this never-before-revealed information will improve their lives. Make the news intriguing enough, and they will read it.

Rule 3: Promise a Benefit in Your Headline

We always want to know, "What's in it for me?" Why should we spend time reading a sales letter, a long email, or pages of web copy? We have to believe we'll discover something that will make us thinner, richer, more popular, free of stress, or something else that will change our lives for the better. Hint at the benefit in the headline, and people will be motivated to read on.

Rule 4: Follow Rules #2 and #3 in Your Headline

If putting news in your headline is powerful and promising a benefit in your headline is powerful, how much more powerful would it be to include both? The answer is: very. It also helps to use certain surefire words and expressions in your headline. Halbert said these are some of the best:

- Announcing
- At last
- Now
- Now, at last
- How to
- Here are
- 17 ways to
- The art of
- The secret of
- A startling fact about
- Amazing
- New

Use these words and phrases strategically in your headlines, and you will increase their pulling power.

One Great Headline

Halbert offered the following headline as one that was as good as money in the bank:

At Last! Scientists Discover New
Way to Look Younger in Just 17 Days!

The first two words, "At Last!", create the impression that this is something people have been waiting to happen for a long time, and the reader will likewise be helped by this great development. The word "Scientists" implies legitimacy. Whatever is going to be reported on in this letter has the backing of the scientific community, and thus can be relied on. The word "Discover" calls up a picture of hard work in a laboratory and scientific breakthroughs, and implies that the reader is going to learn about something real and thoroughly researched. The phrase "New Way" means this is going to be different from all those old ways that we know didn't work, answering the need for "news" in a headline. The words "To Look Younger" are the hook that will capture the interest of every reader. We all want to look younger, unless we're 12 years old. The phrase "In Just 17 Days" is brilliant because it promises quick results, and the number 17 is so specific that it makes the whole promise more believable. The reader thinks, "Why would they give an odd number like 17 unless it were true? Why would you make up a number like that?"

Now, I would hope that a real copywriter producing a headline like this would actually have data in hand from a real scientist validating that amazing results happened in 17 days. In fact, the law probably requires it. For now, though, we won't question the truth of the headline; we're just looking at it for the lessons it can teach us about effective copywriting. From that perspective, this is indeed a great headline.

You Can Learn How to Do This Too

How can YOU learn to write headlines like that? Well, Halbert had a method he used with his own students. He had them copy out his own successful sales letters by hand, word for word. It built a kind of habit of great writing.

He claimed the same approach would work for learning how to write great headlines. He suggested you go to some of the biggest magazines, such as *Reader's Digest*, *People*, *Sports Illustrated*, and so on. Look at the ads, and then write out the headlines onto 3 x 5 index cards, one headline to a card.

Get used to writing out headlines that are obviously good or advertisers wouldn't be spending thousands (maybe hundreds of thousands) of dollars to place them in these magazines. Get a feel for their rhythm and word usage. Not only do you learn how to write, but you now have a file of great headlines you can refer to at any time for ideas and inspiration.

I encourage you again to discover the power of the "swipe file" (which we have referred to before). In my own and Brian's experience, almost all good copywriters have swipe files of ads written by the greatest copywriters of all time. Many of these are available online. Some are free, and there are other comprehensive resources, like Who's Mailing What!, that are subscription based.

Brian reminds me there are also copywriters and marketers today who have all sorts of formulas and even automated systems to help other writers with key phrases and ways to dig deeper and create the best headlines.

HEADLINES BY ANY OTHER NAME

A headline doesn't always have to be the words at the top of a page of copy. In different contexts it can have different forms. We'll look at several of those forms here: email subject lines and banner ads, as well as envelope teaser copy.

Email Subject Lines and Banner Ad Headlines

For those of you who work mostly on the web, the classic rules of writing winning headlines still apply, but their context is different, and you have some special considerations to keep in mind.

In addition to a real headline that may sit at the top of your HTML email, your email subject line is a type of headline that has to get people's attention. And it must really be powerfully motivating because you have to encourage recipients to click and open the email.

All the classic rules apply here, like appealing to prospects' self-interest, promising a benefit, and so on. Using the person's name in the subject line can be very effective. Longer subject lines that give more information work well too. People are growing warier of emails from unknown sources, so it's best to avoid vague and mysterious headlines that might make them too suspicious to open the email. Then you have some specific email marketing issues that must be addressed.

The Rules Regarding Spam

Email subject lines (and in fact all the copy in the email itself) must conform to certain rules or your emails will be labeled spam and end up in junk folders where they'll never be seen. So familiarize yourself with words and phrases that raise red flags. Spam testing programs will let you know if your emails are likely to be rejected.

Working with Different Platforms

There is a wide array of devices on which people read emails and look at websites, so take into account that people might be reading on small screens.

- Your copy may be broken up—sometimes in odd ways. It's important that the break not occur in a peculiar spot or in a way that fails to give critical information.
- You want enough information in the partial headline that does show to make people want to see the rest of the headline and ultimately read your entire email.
- Always test out your subject lines and headlines on devices of different sizes to see whether they work well at getting the message across or if they need to be adjusted.

Making Your Headline Relevant

If you place ads on other sites to get people to click through to your site or order something directly from you, then the headline on your banner ad basically serves the same purpose as the headline on an ad in a publication. Give it the care and attention you would any other headline. Don't use a headline that has no connection to the product or service people see when they arrive at your landing page.

Envelope Teaser Copy

If you're running a direct mail campaign, where you send out your sales piece to large numbers of people via the post office, there are several different kinds of headlines that come into play. There's the headline at the top of the sales letter itself, but if you're sending your letter in an envelope, the first thing your recipient sees won't be the headline. That's when you need to do something clever that will get readers to open that envelope in the first place.

One way is to put teaser copy on the envelope, which is very much like a headline. It's also comparable to putting an enticing subject line on an email to get people to click through. You want it to hint at some kind of benefit the person will receive by opening the envelope. They will find important news, a money-saving coupon, or a solution to some difficulty that's been bothering them. Maybe they'll find the solution to their money problems or a magic elixir that will make them look younger. The copy could consist of one strong line: "Your Free Gift Inside!" Or it could be a strong line with additional points, maybe in the form of bullet points:

Secrets to Financial Success Inside!

Discover:

▮ The easy 3-step process to financial freedom

▮ Four foolproof methods to amass great wealth

▮ How to secure a worry-free retirement

▮ The one financial blunder you should never make

If you are putting copy like this on your envelope, you definitely want to place it on the address side of the envelope. (Some mailers also find it effective to put copy on the other side of the envelope as well.)

Brian says Eugene Schwartz always talked to him about the "real estate" on the envelope, and that he preferred 9-by-12 envelopes to No. 10 business envelopes (which are 4⅛ by 9½) because it gave him so much more space to add compelling copy.

Schwartz never wanted to waste space. He hated white space on his envelopes. That doesn't mean there may not be times when you want to send out large envelopes without a lot of copy on them. But Schwartz's rule of not wasting any white space could be one you want to test.

It always comes down to the same thing, doesn't it? You have to test everything for yourself in your product niche and with your best prospects. And while you're testing, consider another approach altogether.

Some mailers find that making an envelope mysterious and intriguing works best for them. They don't put any copy on the envelope except for a return address with no name. If you do that with a first class stamp or even a bulk live stamp (rather than a printed indicia), many people will think it may be a personal letter. Put it in an envelope with the right shape, and it may even look like an invitation. This may be just what's needed to get prospects to open the envelope, and once they do, your clever headline on the letter itself will lead them right into your sales message.

Brian brought to my attention an example from when he worked at Boardroom Inc. on an estate planning book. One of the copywriters had an idea for an outer envelope that said, in small typewriter font:

Deeply and Irrevocably Personal

When Brian and Marty Edelston tried it, it beat the control, which was heavy on copy, by a huge margin. This test outcome made sense because the new wording was congruent with the intimate subject matter. When it comes to estate planning, "deeply and irrevocably personal" is consistent, whereas a screaming headline on an outer envelope might be a turnoff. This is a good lesson for the need for congruence between your subject matter, how you write your headline, and how much "real estate" you use.

Another idea for an envelope that gets opened is to make it look like an official document, a FedEx letter, or a certified letter. This doesn't fall strictly under the category of headlines, but it is a way to get your prospects' attention, so it serves the same purpose.

Finally, many direct mail campaigns use postcards. A postcard may be small or large, but even the small ones may have two kinds of "headlines." There's the headline on the main copy on the front of the postcard, and there's the teaser copy on the address side of the card. Devote careful attention to both of these important pieces of advertising real estate, and you could have a dynamic postcard that brings huge results.

HEADLINES—YESTERDAY AND TODAY

I hope that as you read these headline rules from all the legends, you are thinking about how you could apply them to your own writing. They apply to every kind of writing, not just writing headlines on ads.

You may need big bold copy that captures people's interest, and that may involve creating a great title for your blog or captivating copy on your website's homepage. Either way, you can use the rules you're learning here to write copy that will get attention and encourage people to spend more time on your site. These rules work, so apply them to whatever you do.

As we've seen, the headline, in its various forms, may be the most important copy in whatever you're writing, so give it the time and attention it deserves. I know professional copywriters who say they spend more time on the headline than any other part of a sales piece.

Try writing a large number of different headlines. Brainstorm ideas until you come upon something that looks really irresistible, and then test it out. This could be the most critical step in creating a winning campaign. If you'd like to see some more history-making ad headlines, visit TheAdvertisingSolution.com and read my article "The Best Headlines of All Time—And What They Can Teach Us Today."

CHAPTER 7

HOW TO BE CREATIVE

OUR LEGENDS GAVE US GREAT INFORMATION on the elements that form the basis of successful marketing materials. In later chapters, we'll look at what they had to say about how we can improve on the performance of what we write by making adjustments that increase the rate of response, but in this chapter, we're going to focus on something much more personal. We're going to look at how you can develop the ability to be creative and write killer copy, blog posts, job applications, or whatever you need.

What is the process a legendary marketer goes through to create these amazing combinations of words that can motivate people to take action? Can you develop the skill to do this as well?

Yes, you can.

In fact, two of our legends were generous and forthcoming in sharing the step-by-step process they followed—a process anyone can emulate. Of course, not everyone can produce marketing campaigns of the caliber created by a Eugene Schwartz or a Gary Halbert. They were in a class by themselves. But anyone can use their methods to improve their skills and produce successful marketing copy. The information they shared is so helpful and encouraging that I know you can use it to enhance all your marketing efforts. You never have to be at a loss for words when you have the guidance of Schwartz and Halbert.

NEVER HAVE WRITER'S BLOCK AGAIN

If you've ever tried to write anything, you know what it's like to face the dreaded blank page or empty computer screen with its infuriating flashing cursor. We'll do anything to avoid it. Suddenly we remember that the dog needs to be walked, the laundry needs to be folded, or it's time for lunch. Any writer will tell you that often the hardest part of writing is just getting started.

Isn't it amazing? Our noisy minds will happily chatter away all day, thinking, judging, and commenting on everything we see. But sit down before a blank sheet with the intention of creating something, and suddenly there's nothing but dead silence.

We call it "writer's block." And this tendency for the mind to go blank and lose touch with any creative impulse has stymied the efforts of many aspiring authors. Whether you're writing a sales piece, a love letter, a memoir, an outline for a speech, or a grant proposal, you'll never succeed if you can't even get the first words out.

Legendary copywriter Eugene Schwartz claimed never to have been plagued by writer's block, and it was for a simple reason: he had developed a surefire method for writing that enabled him to get right to work, without wandering around in that limbo of helplessness. We'll look at this method in detail first, and then we'll look at some other helpful insights Schwartz had to share about creativity and the creative process.

"A Very Simple Way to Make Sure You Get Down to Work"

Schwartz claimed his method for overcoming writer's block was based in Zen principles. I don't know about that, but the process he followed does make a lot of sense. Basically, he found an easy, almost automatic way to get the writing process going that required very little thought or creativity, therefore bypassing any anxiety in the mind of the writer.

Before he actually started writing the copy for an ad, he laid the groundwork with some concentrated but quite easy preparation. As an example of his process, let's suppose it was time for him to work on an ad for one of Rodale's health books. He was one of Rodale's most successful copywriters, and he wrote many of their bestselling sales pieces.

This is how he did it.

He would start by reading the book he was to sell, maybe four times. There's nothing anxiety-provoking or demanding about that. Each time he read through it, he would highlight lines and phrases he thought were important or sounded interesting.

By the time he was finished, a lot of the book would be highlighted. At that point, he'd give the book to his secretary, who would type up all those powerful lines and come back with 40 to 50 pages of words and sentences that came right out of the book.

Now, to make this relevant to you, you may be writing a sales piece about your own book or a blog, or some information about a product you've developed. To follow Schwartz's method, you would simply gather all the information you have about what you're selling in one place, and then go through it just as Schwartz describes, highlighting the critical information and exciting points.

I also realize you likely don't have a secretary to type up all the meaningful text that you pull out from your stock of information, but these days you really don't need one. Since so much of what we do is electronically based, you can just copy and paste anything you want into a new document. You can even speak the text into a dictation program that automatically types everything you say. So it should be easy to adapt Schwartz's method to whatever product you're selling and whatever technology you're using.

Getting back to Schwartz, thanks to reading the book he was selling so many times, he now knew the material backwards and forwards—probably better than any of the book editors who had worked with the author directly. And with all the most powerful lines of the book distilled down into one document, he was ready to go on to the next step.

For this phase of the process, Schwartz always followed the same procedure. He was definitely a creature of habit, and in this case his habits led to an approach that always seemed to work like a charm. He started by bringing up his secretary's typed pages on his computer (well, at least he had a computer, so he wasn't too far back in the dark ages). The information on these pages would form the vocabulary of the final sales piece. Then he would pour himself a cup of coffee, mix it with cream and sugar—the same way every day—and place his pad and pencil in the same place in front of him each time. He would set his timer for 33:33—33 minutes and 33 seconds—the amount of time a person can best focus attention.

And then he'd hit the start button.

For the next 33 minutes and 33 seconds he would sit there. The rules were that he could do anything he wanted during that time, as long as it related to the copy. He could ignore it or work on it, but he could not do anything else. He could not read another book, write a letter, play with any gadgets he might have on his desk, make a phone call, or get up from his chair. He did not even try to write a great sales piece, nor would he allow himself to think about the money he'd make by creating a great sales piece. For those 33 minutes and 33 seconds, he had no goal or responsibility to himself or the client, other than to sit there and relate to the copy.

Eventually he'd get bored. Wouldn't you? So he'd start looking at the copy staring back at him from his computer screen. As he scrolled through the pages, some sentences would catch his attention. He'd feel no writer's block or anxiety because he wasn't really doing anything but reading the copy and allowing it to tell him what to do.

Some sentences would look like they belonged together, so he'd move them around, putting them into different categories of copy that would later become the different sections of the final piece he would create. These categories might include things like opening copy, closing copy, ailments and solutions, success stories and testimonials, expert tips, etc.

Occasionally some combination of powerful or intriguing words that looked like they might be the basis of a great headline would jump out, so he'd move that to the top. Other combinations would jump out that looked like subheads, which could be used as lead-ins to the different categories he was forming, so he'd move those words into place. Some copy would look like it could be separated out to make a good sidebar (like a list of five super foods for vibrant health). As he went along, he'd fix some awkward wording or polish the copy a little if it seemed obvious to him, but he wouldn't do any real writing.

Then, after 33:33, the timer would go off. He'd stop right where he was, even in mid-sentence, and take a break. During the break, he would stand up from his desk for five minutes of "compulsory leisure." He could get another cup of coffee, play with the dog—do anything but work on the sales piece.

When break time was over, he'd go back to his computer and do the same thing again for another 33:33. He'd do this for four or five hours a day.

Can you see how easy this is, and why he would never suffer any writer's block?

He was never actually writing the way we think: someone sitting down and attempting to create brilliant copy out of his own mind. In fact, he believed that trying to create brilliant copy out of the imagination was a sure way to create copy that wouldn't convince anyone of anything.

All he was doing was sifting through the material he'd already gleaned from the book, rearranging it, and highlighting the best points. In a way, the piece was writing itself. He was just facilitating the process.

Isn't this a completely new view of the writing process? Doesn't it sound like something you could do?

Granted, it was Schwartz's genius eye that enabled him to pick out the best copy, recognize the brilliant headline, and put it all together to create an irresistible sales message. Once he had everything organized, he could go in and add great turns of phrase and connecting copy that would put the finishing touches on the piece.

You can see how using his method would eliminate the fearsome writer's block—those awful hours of just sitting there doing nothing. It seems that anyone who really loved and knew his or her product or service could use this method to pull together all the elements needed to create an amazing sales piece. Brian shared an observation that many have made: "Gene Schwartz assembled copy, rather than simply writing it."

According to Brian, Schwartz followed the same procedure when he worked on Boardroom's copy:

1. He'd go through the books using the underlining process.
2. He'd figure out which items were the edgiest and most exciting, and he'd bring those up to the top of the letter into the headlines and subheads.
3. Then he'd assemble the entire mail piece from everything he'd gleaned from his reading.

However, this was just the beginning. Until now, Schwartz had worked on the piece just by pulling information out of the words that were already set out before him. Once he finished this phase, he was ready to go on to the next.

He was about to "create."

"How Does One Create?"

Schwartz believed that creativity was a habit that could be cultivated so that it became automatic. In order to understand how this process worked, one first had to understand the nature of the human mind as Schwartz saw it.

According to research he had studied on how the brain works, we are able to focus our attention on our conscious mind, but that mind is only capable of holding about seven memory bytes. That's a very narrow range of possibility. It works very well on logical syllogisms and figuring out the consequences of our actions, but that's not creation.

The act of true creation is to create something out of nothing. As Schwartz said:

Only God can do that, and we're only human.

So instead of talking about the idea of human creation, Schwartz talked about human connectivity. He said that the genius of the human mind is its ability to make connections between things in new ways. We can take two separate thoughts and bring them together under a connecting umbrella so that one thought is formed out of two. We don't have to create something that never existed before (an impossibility). We just have to connect things in a way they've never been connected before. This is what it means to have something new:

New—in every discipline—means never joined before.

Schwartz didn't believe we could do this with our conscious minds. The connections are made outside our consciousness. So what we have to do is trick the conscious mind by focusing it on something simple, such as making a cup of coffee. While the conscious mind is occupied with this straightforward task, the unconscious mind can start making connections that will seep into the back of our conscious mind and then work their way to the front, where we become aware of them.

Remember, this isn't creating anything new, but making new connections between what already exists. Schwartz claimed he made the best connections and got his best ideas while shaving. He was always open and ready for these revelations to occur, and he would just write down them down as they came to him.

Then all he had to do was integrate these new connections into the copy he had been working on—all those reorganized ideas and headlines and subheads he had pulled from the pages his secretary had typed up.

By now he was completely immersed in his subject matter. With his deepening understanding of the product's unique features, maybe something would now jump out at him as the best headline, which he could then tweak by adding an image that came to him while he was shaving. Or perhaps it would become clear to him how to organize the copy for the best flow. The sales piece would begin to form itself.

Two Critical Points That Made Eugene Schwartz One of the Best Copywriters of His Era

If we were to summarize Schwartz's two main points for a stress-free, blockage-free approach to writing winning copy, they would be:

1. *Work harder than anyone else.* That doesn't mean straining your brain trying to be creative. It means going over your material again and again to see what pops out. He said that on the sixth reading, you'll finally see the best material that's been in there the entire time, just waiting for you to tease it out.
2. *Get down to work.* That can be difficult when you're feeling anxious and pressured to do a good job, and you want to be anywhere but sitting in front of that blank page. But you can avoid this problem by using Schwartz's simple techniques to get working and trick yourself—and your unconscious brain—into being "creative."

The system obviously worked for him. His success proved it, and I have no doubt that it can work for you too.

GARY HALBERT'S "MOST IMPORTANT TECHNIQUE" FOR WRITING COPY

Now let's move along to Gary Halbert's advice on how to get the creative juices flowing. As we saw in Chapter 6, Halbert believed that not only studying but actually copying out successful ads by hand was one of the best ways for a new copywriter to develop his or her craft.

Many of his students who tried this method did in fact go on to become great copywriters in their own right. It seems that doing this exercise played a role in training the brain—or, at least, that's what Halbert believed. Whatever the reason, he appears to have been a great teacher, so perhaps he was correct about the efficacy of this method.

Another of Halbert's methods for learning how to become a good writer was to write. If you never write, you'll never learn how. If you just sit down and start writing, without worrying about grammar, syntax, punctuation, or perfection, you'll learn by doing. With time, you're bound to become better at it.

In one of his famous newsletters, Halbert revealed what he called "the most powerful and important technique of all when it comes to writing copy." We'll look at it in some depth here. The basis of Halbert's technique was his belief that you'd never be able to write great copy by using your imagination—the same lesson we heard from Eugene Schwartz.

Halbert believed that in order to be really successful, you have to find out as much as you can about your prospects: who they are and what they want. With that intimate knowledge, you can gear your copy to be specifically in alignment with the interests, needs, and values of the people you are trying to sell your product or service to. He summed up the concept in the following haiku-like instruction:

More Answers Will Be Found
Through Movement Than
Will Ever Be Found Through
Meditation

As you will recall, Schwartz said the writing method he used was based on Zen principles. Perhaps Halbert was similarly inspired. Halbert said that deliberately trying to be clever and creative, to "dream up" an ad that would work, was a very dumb way to approach writing. You couldn't possibly make up something in your head that would work. Really great copywriters are willing to "become intimately involved" with the people they are trying to sell to.

They actively seek those people out (the "movement" in the above instruction). They want to talk with their prospects, meet with them, and discover the secrets of their hearts and minds. Only from that knowledge will great copy flow. It will not necessarily sound clever, but it will be powerful copy that speaks directly to prospects' desires and motivate them to order the product.

To help copywriters accomplish this, Halbert suggested five steps they should follow that progressively lead to closer interaction with prospects and the discovery of what it takes to sell them a product. Some of these steps may seem pretty extreme, and some may sound a bit outdated, but their overall message is still useful and adaptable.

If you're a business owner, blogger, or website creator who is trying your hand at writing for the first time, this is an ideal program to follow. Be aware that Halbert primarily wrote sales pieces for direct mail campaigns, so his ideas are slanted to that application. Even so, there's a lot here that can help anyone in the business of selling a product or promoting a person or a cause. So let's look at Halbert's technique for writing better copy, as summed up in these five steps.

"Step #1: Get a Printout of the Names and Addresses of Your Customers and Best Prospects and Then Sit Down and Read That Printout"

When you run a direct mail campaign, you may rent a list of names and addresses through a list manager or broker. This list is carefully selected to contain the names of individuals who have perhaps bought products like yours in the past or who fall into a certain demographic that you believe contains prospective buyers. Or you may have collected your own list of people who have already bought from you or who have inquired about your product or service. This is the kind of printout Halbert was talking about.

Even if most of your work is online, you may have a list of email addresses you bought from a broker or gathered yourself. Hopefully you also have these individuals' names and home addresses. You may even have their telephone numbers and other demographic information. You can certainly adapt Halbert's method to this kind of list as well.

If you're writing a job or college application, his approach can be adapted to this task as well. It's really just a series of steps you use to find out as much as possible about your target audience so you can plan your most powerful message.

Halbert started with a regular mailing list. First he looked at the composition of the people on the list. Are there more men or women? Do the names indicate that the people tend to belong to one particular ethnic group? Are they Latino? Asian? Are they the type of people who use their full names, or do they tend to use initials? Do they have professional titles, like doctor or professor?

Next he looked at the addresses. What part of the country do they favor? Do they live in big cities or in rural areas? Do they live in apartments, multifamily dwellings, or single-family homes? What kind of neighborhoods do they live in? If you know the area well yourself, you can tell by the names of the cities and towns. If you don't know the area, you can research the demographics of different zip codes. That will tell you if people tend to be wealthier or poorer. Do they live in upscale apartments or in public housing?

After reading Halbert's description of how he looked at such a list and all the information he could glean from it about who was buying a product, I felt I was watching a genius at work. Can you believe all the gold you can get just by looking at mailing labels? But that's just the beginning. Let's move on to Step #2.

"Step #2: Look at the Mail You Receive from Your Customers"

If your company receives mail from people, it is very instructive to look at it. Don't even read the mail at this point (that comes later). For now, just look at it. This may not work for you if most of your customer interactions are over the phone or by email. Still, even a few letters or returned order forms may be instructive, although they will probably represent a limited sample of your customer base.

You can tell if letters come from a computer printer or if they're handwritten. Do they have the spidery handwriting of an elderly person, or is the writing firm and robust? Are letters written on expensive stationery, or are they written on a sheet torn off a yellow pad? Is the return address label a freebie from Easterseals?

If people mail in orders, do they pay with cash, money orders, stamps (people actually sometimes paid with stamps back when Halbert gave this advice!), credit cards, or checks? If it's a check, is it written from a joint account or a single-owner account? And is it a plain check, or is it illustrated with kittens or American flags? You're beginning to get a clearer picture of who your best customers are. You'll learn more if you go on to Step #3.

"Step #3: Now Start Reading Your Mail, and Start Taking Telephone Calls from Your Business Customers"

Now actually read those letters, and find out what people are writing about. Are they writing to make a complaint? Are they making requests for a certain kind of information? Are they suggesting something they would like to see from you that would improve their experience with your company or product? This will show you what's important to them and give you clues as to what features of your product and service to stress in your marketing materials.

You'll learn even more if you talk to customers when they call in with orders, complaints, or questions. Turn the moment around by asking them questions. Why did they buy the product? What did they like or dislike? Why are they returning it? What would make the product better?

Then try to upsell them so you can find out what techniques work best. Is offering a discount effective? Or is it better to offer them a buy-two-get-one-free deal? This will teach you how to best position your offer in your sales pieces.

You've learned a lot of valuable information by following Halbert's Steps 1 through 3. Only the really dedicated will dare to try Step #4.

"Step #4: Start Making Telephone Calls to Your Customers"

If you're willing to reach out to your customers and call them on the phone, you can really get some great information. What Halbert suggests is to first send a letter to 100 of your best customers with a dollar bill attached to the top of your first page. (Remember, that was Collier's suggestion for getting people to take notice—and it always worked for him!)

In the letter, tell the customer that you enclosed the dollar bill to get his attention because you have something important to tell him, and then include the important information in the letter. This means you should plan to have something newsworthy to share with the customer—perhaps a new product or a change or improvement to your service.

Then, several days later, call and remind him of the letter. Thanks to the dollar bill, if he did see the letter he will surely remember it, and now you're in a great position to start a conversation. Halbert said that if you ask the right questions, you will be able to learn more about what your customers want—and how best to sell them your product—than a thousand creative types who are writing from their imaginations.

Admittedly, Step #4 requires a bit of gumption. Most people don't feel comfortable calling up a bunch of strangers. But only the most courageous will move on to Step #5, and I don't necessarily recommend you follow it, but here it is nonetheless.

"Step #5: Go Out to Where Your Customers Live, and Knock on Their Front Door, and Ask If You Can Come in and Talk To Them"

This is pretty extreme, and it's unlikely many will do this. If you do follow through on it, sitting at someone's kitchen table will certainly show you firsthand how your customers live. It will give you the opportunity to find out exactly what they want, and you'll get a pretty good idea how to tell them what they want to hear so they make the decision to buy. Halbert explained why you should take any or all of these steps:

> When it comes to writing great copy, it is not so much a matter of knowing how to write as it is of knowing what to write.

You won't know what to write until you know who you're writing to, what they really want, and what sells them the best. Halbert's point was that if you learn everything you can about your customer, the writing will take care of itself.

One of the big lessons for you to take away from all this is that "one size fits all" copy is never a good idea. If you're going to create different packages for different niches, which I highly recommend, you also want to create different copy for different list segments. Always keep in mind that you don't have just one homogeneous list. There are many sublists within your big list, and Halbert teaches us that you must write to everybody.

Brian likes to say, "There are no unique names; only unique lists."

We manage this in direct mail, so there's no excuse not to do it online, where it's even easier. Writing copy to specific list segments will increase response rates across the board, so you'll find the effort is well worth it.

THE KEY TO CREATIVITY IS KNOWLEDGE

Both Schwartz and Halbert offered us very practical steps for writing great marketing materials. Their methods were very different, but in essence they were both saying the same thing: Don't worry so much about being creative. Pay attention to building your knowledge, and what you should say will be given to you.

Schwartz said to focus on finding out everything you can about the product. Gather together all your information, sift through it, rearrange it, let your subconscious go to work, and a great piece of sales copy will emerge.

Halbert said to focus on finding out everything you can about your target audience. Find out who they are, what interests them, and what they want, and your sales copy will be directed by that.

A critical point both of them made is that it never works to start "creating" based on things you dream up about your product or your audience. It may result in something that sounds good on the surface, but is unlikely to persuade anyone to do anything. Your sales material must be based in reality or it just won't work.

So what does all this mean when you are trying to write a great grant proposal, a winning cover letter for a job application, or an inspiring blog that will reach troubled teens, new mothers, or gourmet chefs?

1. *Gather as much information as you can about your product.* Do it even if you are the product. Don't get anxious or concerned during this part of the process. Just put together everything you know and then go over and over that material until things jump out at you and start telling a story.

2. *Find out as much as you can about your target audience.* Is it a university committee? A corporate human resources department? A group of amateur sports buffs or young career women? Discover what interests them, what language they use, what their problems are, and what they're willing to do to resolve their difficulties. If possible, you may even want to take a tip from Halbert and actually go out and talk to them or people who know them. Get the information firsthand if possible.

3. *Put it all together.* Now you know the story you want to tell, and you know the audience you need to tell it to. All the information is right there in front of you. Start putting the pieces together to present your best arguments.

After you have all the material organized and your main points made, you can go back and start polishing. The hard work is already done, and you're well on your way to success.

CHAPTER 8

HOW TO BOOST YOUR RESPONSE TO EVERY AD

ONE CRITICAL SECRET TO SUCCESS, no matter what you do, is to never rest on your laurels—even if you've just run the best promotional campaign ever and you think you've hit on the golden key. For one thing, we never come to the end of our capacity to grow, and therefore we can always do better.

So why settle for less when you can have more?

Plus . . .

▌ *The world doesn't give us much chance to rest on our laurels*. Things are always changing. People, ideas, and images quickly and unexpectedly come in and out of fashion. Your target audience may change their interests and what they want.

▌ *Your competition is always changing the playing field.* They may even be copying you, which means you have to keep coming up with something new and different to stay ahead of the game.

These are the facts of business and life that our legends understood well.

Even though they may have produced the most successful marketing materials of their time, they were always looking for ways to improve on their results and increase the level of response. Part of the science of producing great promotions is to always be working on the next big idea.

In this chapter, we're going to look at advice on changes you can make to your promotions to increase their effectiveness from three of our legends: Robert Collier, John Caples, and Gary Halbert. Let's see what secrets they have to reveal about building better and better campaigns.

"TAKING THE GUESS OUT OF ADVERTISING"

We'll start with Robert Collier. He was a master of writing direct mail copy that elicited a huge response from readers, and he provided us with very helpful explanations of how he came to write his sales letters—the nuts and bolts of what made them work so well.

Although the language he used is a bit old-fashioned for our taste today, and the kinds of items he sold may seem strange to us now, his understanding of the art of persuasion was unequaled. Collier understood that writing advertising copy (or any form of persuasive material, for that matter) needs to be something of a science. It has to get a certain result, and since the success of a business is riding on that result, it's critical that the process be more than a guessing game. It has to be based on facts, testing, and comparing outcomes.

Collier liked to refer to the work of the Tested Selling Institute and Word Laboratory Inc., a company located in New York at the time, which identified words and phrases salespeople could use to get customers to buy. The founder of the institute, Elmer Wheeler, put together a list of 100,000 selling phrases from more than 200 industries and came up with a number of sentences that had proved to be responsible for numerous sales in the field.

He called them "Tested Selling Sentences." These were sentences to primarily be used by salespeople in one-on-one interactions with customers. Salesmen would memorize these sentences and sprinkle them as needed into their sales patter. Wheeler's argument was, "Why gamble with unknown sales phraseology? Why not take advantage of modern science?"

Collier believed that taking this kind of approach to selling would be just as effective when applied to the printed word. For example, his research showed that in writing sales pieces, there were certain tested openings to letters that would invariably win readers' attention, which, of course, is the first step to making a sale.

Of all these openings, the word "How" seemed to work the best. In some cases, using the word "How" in a headline could greatly increase the pull of a sales piece. This rule is certainly still used widely today, as "how" frequently appears in headlines, blog posts, and article titles.

This magic word seems to work no matter what product is being sold. People want practical solutions to their problems, and the word "How" is an immediate signal that, if they will just spend a few minutes reading a sales piece or web page, they will be sure to learn something that will improve their lives.

According to Collier, other "magic" words that impelled people to give their attention and ultimately buy were:

▌ Truth
▌ Life
▌ Love
▌ At last
▌ New
▌ Advice
▌ Facts you should know about . . .

If you read magazines or surf the internet today, you'll find these words popping up again and again. They seem to be as powerful as ever.

The Value of Feeding Vanity

Another principle Collier referred to many times because—as he put it, it "took the guess" out of advertising—is to appeal to readers' vanity. For example, giving the impression that the reader has been specially selected to receive an offer because of his or her unique qualities can lead to a huge response. This approach is used a great deal today. The word "exclusive" appears everywhere, and people still have a positive response to it.

Here's an example from a letter Collier wrote to appeal to his readers' vanity:

> *I Wonder If You Can Qualify as a "Player Patron"?*
>
> *Dear Mr. Jones:*
>
> *You have been designated as one qualified to serve on our Board of "Player Patrons," and our Directors have authorized me to invite you to become one of this select group of amateur sportsmen.*

A variation on this approach is to play up the common desire we all have to feel important. We all like to feel we are necessary. If a sales letter or other promotional material can subtly feed a person's vanity, it can pull a huge response. Here's the opening of another Collier letter that brought amazingly high returns:

> *I Wonder If You Would Be Good Enough to Give Me the Benefit of Your Experience?*
>
> *Dear Sportsman:*
>
> *Will you give me the benefit of your judgment on a matter of considerable importance to us?*

The letter went on to ask readers to give editorial feedback on their magazine, but the real purpose of the letter was to sell subscriptions, which it did very well.

Can you think of ways to play up to your readers' egos with the aim of clinching a sale, getting them to sign up for your newsletter, or getting them to join your website? Make them feel that only people who are discerning, are properly ambitious, or have finer tastes can realize the value of what you offer. They will want to prove they have those qualities by doing what you want them to do.

Successful Letter Openings

Collier gave a number of examples of ways to open letters that proved to work very well.

Here are two of my favorites.

Do Me a Favor

One company he knew of received a great response with letters that began "I wonder if you would be good enough to do me a favor?" It worked so well they started all their letters using those words.

"Give Me ___ and I'll Give You ___"

Collier also found great success with variations on the idea "Give me Five Minutes, and I'll Give You [this or that]." For example, "Give Me Two Minutes—and I'll Give You the Secret of a Goodly Profit Without Investment." Another successful opener to a letter selling a new set of books was: "Give Me Five Days—and I'll Give You the Secret of Learning Any Subject!" Or there was this one: "Give Me 5 Days, and I'll Give You Relief from Itching Feet."

You can see how easy it is to take a good idea like this and adapt it as needed to different subjects. You just have to keep testing it and examining the response rate to make sure the approach is still working. I think these words from Collier explain the process very well:

> The one thing that should always be borne in mind is that it is not merchandise you are selling, but human nature, human reactions. The movie people have found that people always respond to certain motivations, so they have their guaranteed laugh producers, their guaranteed methods of turning on the tears, and so on. . . .
>
> In the same way, you can take an approach that has successfully sold a set of books, and with very little change, adapt it

to selling shoes or socks or luggage or any one of a thousand other products—and be just as successful in disposing of these!

So it's just a question of finding the keys that "take the guess out of advertising," and then applying them to whatever product you're selling. The keys work because they have more to do with human nature than they do with merchandise. As Collier said:

A knowledge of your product is essential, of course. But familiarity with human reactions, human responses to familiar stimuli, is even more important.

It always seems to come back to the same thing, doesn't it? You have to understand your audience. What are people's hidden desires and motivations? Figure out what they are, and then gear your promotions to appeal to those aspects of human nature. Once you find one thing that works, then keep adjusting and adapting and testing what you do so that you get a better and better response with each new campaign.

Sugarcoating the Pill

In addition to using the right words, another way to "take the guess" out of advertising is to sugarcoat the offer by throwing in a bonus or premium. Collier described advertising as:

. . . a matter of making people want some one thing you have, more than they want the money it costs them.

The cost becomes easier to swallow when a special gift is included in the deal. This approach works with just about anything you're selling, from magazine subscriptions to dental implants. Always offer some special bonus, and you can see a huge increase in your rate of response.

If you're new to marketing, or feel you should be getting a better response to your offers, you should think about how to incorporate a bonus. Suppose you want people to subscribe to your blog on financial predictions. Perhaps there's a yearly fee and you wonder if potential subscribers will be put off by that. You can sugarcoat the pill by offering a free book to new or renewing subscribers. Really emphasize how much they will benefit by reading and using the information in the book. You'll probably find that sign-ups increase.

Brian shared with me a situation that came up at Boardroom Inc., where they offered four premium books as part of an offer for a larger book. They kept testing the number of premiums to include in the package, starting with four and then working up to ten, then 50, and finally 100.

They found that each time they added more premiums (which were basically two-page reports, all bound in one book), they increased response and sales. Each addition beat the previous version by a wide margin. These premiums seemed to add a lot of extra value to buyers, without greatly increasing Boardroom's cost.

You have to test it for yourself, of course, but in general, more is better. People want to get something for nothing, so you should always try to create the most irresistible offer you can. If you can give them more without adding too much to your own cost, it could really pay off.

But don't stop there.

Try offering a different book and compare results. If you've managed to move your buyers to an online platform, test the difference between offering a hard-copy book vs. an e-book; the latter will cost you much less to provide, but people may prefer it because they can receive it immediately. Do the testing to find out what works best with your target audience.

Conversely, if you start your marketing online, don't underestimate the perceived value of a "hard premium" (not something digital) to add to the richness of the offer. Even people who are on their computers all day have mailboxes, and if you can capture their physical address, you can expand the ways you can communicate with them and deliver quality information and products.

As Collier taught us, human nature doesn't change. There are certain ways you can approach people that really do "take the guess" out of advertising.

You've been given some of the most effective rules here, but the only way you can find out what works best for you is through testing your own sales pieces and other promotional materials. Once you discover what works, you can use it again and again for better and better results.

CAPLES' 32 WAYS TO GET MORE RESPONSES TO YOUR DIRECT MAIL SALES PIECES

Now we'll move on to John Caples, whose direct mail ads, written in the early 20th century, were hugely successful. We would all do well to listen to any advice from Caples on how to create more effective sales pieces. Fortunately for those of us writing copy today, Caples revealed some of his best secrets in his classic book, *Tested Advertising Methods*. One of the chapters in the book, "Thirty-Two Ways to Get More Inquiries from Your Advertising," is a treasure trove of helpful information. I thought it would be well worth it to list all of these here, with some brief comments.

(*Note*: These methods will work online, too—but of course there was no internet back then.)

Much of this advice is for a very specific purpose: to increase inquiries about a product by offering the target audience some kind of free bonus. As we've just seen, this is a common device used by many current advertisers and is an expansion on Collier's idea of sugarcoating the pill.

The degree to which Caples' advice applies to all media today is amazing. Go over this power-packed list and master its principles, and you'll know that whatever you're promoting and whatever means you're using to reach your target audience (direct mail, email, website copy, Facebook ads), you'll have the best chance of yielding the results you want.

These first ten items from Caples' list refer to the bonus itself:

1. *Mention the offer in the headline.* People are more likely to read your sales piece (or email or website copy) if they're told right at the beginning what's in it for them. That's

why the headline "Learn How to Get Your Free Report on Surefire Weight Loss Methods" will get a bigger response than "Surefire Weight Loss Methods."

2. *Emphasize the word "Free."* If you're offering something at no cost—even if it's just a bonus item included with purchase—make the most of that appealing fact. The word "free" is one of the most powerful words in any ad. One way to make sure it gets noticed is to put it in a "burst" as a graphic element in a prominent place. If you're online, you can even have the word flash on and off so it really catches the eye.

3. *Mention the offer in a subhead.* One effective way to arrange the beginning of your sales piece or the top part of your web page is to have a strong headline followed by a subhead that presents the offer. This breaks the offer down into easily digestible bites, which makes it more likely that readers will get the message. For example:

Learn Surefire Weight Loss Methods

Get Your FREE Book by Responding in 72 Hours!

4. *Show a picture of the booklet or sample.* A picture can be worth ten thousand words. Show a picture of what you're giving away with a "Free" burst displayed prominently, and readers will quickly get the idea.

5. *Mention the offer in the first paragraph.* Don't wait until the end of the piece to describe what you're giving away. Readers may not get that far if they're not motivated to keep going. Describe attractive parts of the offer from the outset to keep people reading. You don't have to give them all the details at this point, but tell them enough to capture their interest. Then promise that if they keep reading, you'll tell them more later. In an online ad, place the information "above the fold" where it can be seen without having to scroll.

6. *Use an attractive booklet title.* The title of the booklet you're giving away as a bonus is part of your ad copy. The

title itself should offer a benefit, such as "Five Easy Steps to Losing Weight," or "Beauty Secrets That Will Make You Look Ten Years Younger." If you're giving away a product, you may not be able to change its name, but you can add a benefit to its name with a strong adjective, such as Age-Defying Princessa Face Cream, or Muscle-Maximizing Atlas Protein Powder.

7. *Include an attractive description of the offer.* Make a list of all the good things about your giveaway product. For example, if it's a free booklet, offer a list of bullet points (e.g., five easy steps, illustrated, complete instructions). A table of contents could also be appealing since it's a quick summary of everything the book contains.

8. *Include a booklet foreword by a famous person.* If you can associate your booklet with someone your readers have heard of and admire, it will increase the perceived value of your offer. So if your book of golfing tips has a foreword by a famous golfer or your book of beauty tips has a foreword by a movie star or supermodel, that's worth highlighting in your sales piece.

9. *Include testimonials.* Testimonials from experts in the field, admired celebrities, or people just like your readers who benefited from the booklet or product will make your bonus seem more "legitimate" and worthwhile. Especially today, when people use social networking to talk about their experiences with products they use, we've come to rely on the opinions of others. Testimonials are a very powerful way to influence people. Of course, if you're selling yourself in a job application, your list of references is also like a set of testimonials, so use them well.

10. *Sweeten your offer.* The more items you add to your offer, the more tempting it will be (as we discussed above in "Sugarcoating the Pill"). Add another bonus, and it will make the offer even more attractive. For example, you can add a second booklet, a free sample, or a free consultation

(a great opportunity to sell more). Pile on the benefits, and people will be more likely to respond.

TV offers are notorious for this. They'll throw in more and more items, and then they'll double the entire offer. These people know what they're doing, so take your cue from them.

And remember, sometimes it's a matter of how you present your offer. If you're giving away a pack of makeup samples, don't just present it as a single package. List them as individual items; it will make it sound like a bigger bonus.

11. *Include a coupon.* A coupon is a visual call to action. Even if people call or go online rather than mailing in their order—and even if the coupon is only a graphic on a web page—just seeing the coupon can get them moving. Also, the discount the coupon offers is a benefit that reduces the risk of making a purchase.

12. *Print the value on the coupon.* Don't expect readers to do the math. If you offer a 25-percent-off coupon, clearly state "Up to a $25 value"—or whatever it happens to be. The coupon will appear to be as valuable as money, and therefore something worth following up on.

13. *Include some selling copy on the coupon.* Every inch of space on your sales piece, your email, or your website is valuable real estate, including the coupon. So repeat the offer, the value, and the guarantee right there on the coupon. Even if readers look at nothing but the coupon, they should still get a good idea of the offer.

14. *Print your address twice in each ad.* This is especially important for direct mail sales pieces. Don't depend upon your reader to go hunting for your contact information. Make it easy to find. In fact, you could print it at the bottom of every page, and put it prominently near your call to action.

Don't forget to include your phone number and address on everything you send out, regardless of its format. Make sure all the relevant contact information is prominently displayed on your emails, web pages, blog posts, or anything else you present to the public.

15. *Include a telephone number—especially a toll-free number.* This is even more true today than when Caples wrote this advice. Make sure you provide an easy way for people to reach you that won't cost them anything.

   It seems that 800 phone numbers are often a forgotten "response device" in a world of URLs and email, but everyone who is on a computer all day also has a telephone. Even though most people have phone plans that don't charge anything extra for long-distance calls, they still respond favorably to toll-free numbers, so use one if you can.

16. *Spotlight "Fax for Ordering"—make it toll-free.* In Caples' day, the fax machine was a new technology. You may not use a fax number as a way for people to contact you, but the more general principle is to use whatever technology is available to give people a convenient way to reach you—and make it free!

17. *Emphasize "No Obligation."* People don't want to take a risk, so keep assuring them that there is no obligation and nothing to lose. State your guarantee, and keep repeating that they are taking no risks by ordering from you, subscribing to your website, etc. The words "Money-Back Guarantee" are very powerful.

   Also, it helps to tell people that their private information will never be shared with others (assuming that's true and you will not be selling names). Most websites have privacy policies in which they explain exactly what they do, and don't do, with the information they collect.

18. *Offer certain information in a plain envelope.* If the information you're offering may be embarrassing to people (like information on personal hygiene products), assure readers it will arrive in a plain envelope. This will help remove some hesitation they may have about ordering.

People want their privacy protected online as well, although it's not as easy to ensure that as it is when you're working with an envelope. Embarrassing subject lines will get a prospect to delete an email just as quickly as a direct mail customer would throw out an embarrassing envelope.

19. *Urge immediate action.* If people don't act right away, they may never respond at all, so give them a reason to act immediately. Put a time limit on the offer, say supplies are limited, etc.

20. *Include a business-reply postcard.* If you can afford it, including a postage-paid postcard or envelope in your direct mail package can increase response rates. It also increases your costs, so do a cost-benefit analysis to see if the increased inquiries (and ultimate sales) make up for the greater initial outlay on your part.

    Obviously, when marketing online we don't run into this problem of "cost to respond," but if you are dealing with a physical product, offering to pay the shipping and handling is a nice way to sweeten the deal.

21. *Include a fold-over coupon.* This is a way of providing a business-reply device that costs the mailer less to produce and costs the buyer nothing to mail. Again, the takeaway for us is to try to use whatever technology is currently available to give buyers a cost-free way to respond.

22. *Use a freestanding insert.* If you're sending out a direct mail package, you can include a lift note or a single-page or multiple-page ad within your larger sales piece, in the same envelope if you're using one. This will get attention and give you an opportunity to provide more information or reiterate your offer. Again, do a cost-benefit analysis to determine whether the increased cost pays off in increased response.

    The online version of this is to develop different pages on your website providing different types of information, such as "About Us," "Case Histories," or "Testimonials." Make sure every part of your website is doing a good job of persuading visitors to take the action you want them to take.

23. *Test several different offers.* Never assume you know what your target audience wants. Test several different bonuses, samples, or booklet titles. Test different ways for people to get back to you (phone call, ordering online, etc.). See what gives you the biggest response.

   However, be careful about presenting multiple offers in the same promotion because that often depresses response rates. Too many choices make people think too much and may give them a reason to put off ordering, which often leads to the loss of the sale. If you have multiple ordering options, be sure to test response in comparison to a single offer to see whether offering too many choices is hurting you.

   Also, when looking for a winning offer, try to do "single variable testing" whenever possible. That means testing one thing at a time so you know what's either lifting or reducing response. If you test too many variables at one time without isolating them, it's almost impossible to figure out how each change contributed to the final outcome.

24. *Test several different ads.* Whether it's a direct mail sales piece or a web page, vary headlines, formats, or sales piece lengths. Test several possibilities to see which yields the biggest response. Even if the ad you're using now seems to be working great, you should always be creating and testing something new. This way, if your current ad suddenly stops getting the response you want, you won't be left with any downtime.

25. *Use the most effective media.* Your product and your target audience will determine which medium works best. Should you promote online? Through direct mail? Through broadcast media? Only testing will tell you where you get the most bang for your buck.

26. *Skim the cream from various markets.* This is related to the previous point, but it concerns using the most effective

markets within one medium. For example, which website is the best host for your banner ads? Does that vary by season? One website may work so well for you that you'll want to advertise on it continuously. Another website may give spotty results but work well for occasional sales. Moving around from site to site may put your message before fresh eyes, and ads in print media may sometimes work well. As Caples told us:

This system of shifting media is something like fishing. The experienced fisherman shifts from one location to another in order to catch more fish.

But as he would also tell us—test everything! And don't confine yourself to one medium. This is sage advice for today's marketers as well.

27. *Use the most effective space size.* Regardless of the medium, sometimes a large ad works best. Sometimes, though, a smaller ad will yield an equal number of responses with less strain on your advertising budget.

28. *Use long copy.* Research shows that the more information you give people about a product, the greater the response you will receive. So whatever size ad you use, make sure it's filled with copy. Give plenty of facts and benefits to convince people to take you up on your offer. Make it easy for them to make the decision you want.

29. *Use the best season.* Certain times are better for offering promotions than others, and you should allocate your advertising budget accordingly. For his mail order ads, Caples found he got the best response in the winter and a depressed response in the summer. He also found that when placing newspaper ads, the day of the week was critical. It may be different now, so once again, find out through testing which season works best for you.

30. *Use the best-pulling positions in publications.* This advice from Caples referred specifically to print media advertising.

If you're promoting a product related to cooking or eating out, place the ad in the food section. If you're promoting a concert or sporting event, place the ad in the entertainment section. In general, try to place your ad in the upper-right-hand corner of the right-hand page, which is the most visible spot.

This is common sense, and it applies to advertising on websites as well. Place your ad on the website pages that attract people who will be interested in what you're selling, and get it above the fold so they will see it even if they don't scroll down.

31. *Study the offerings of your competitors.* You don't have to reinvent the wheel. See what your competitors are doing, especially if you're just starting out. How long is their copy? What kind of offer are they making? If they're successful, you can get some ideas from them to give yourself a leg up. For example, if they're sending out a 12-page magalog, consider using the same format for your direct mail ad. If they have a video message on their website, try producing one yourself.

Don't just imitate them, though. Make it your aim to outdo them. Don't copy them word for word. Come up with new wording or a better angle. Explain how much more superior your product is compared to theirs. Let your competitors inspire you to be better.

Brian reminds me, given his experience working with some of the greatest copywriters who ever lived, of "the power of swipe files"—files filled with successful ads you should refer to for ideas and inspiration. Throughout this book, the fact that we've quoted great headlines and letter openings from our legends tells you how dedicated we are to studying the past. For you, that should include the offerings of your competitors.

32. *Keep records of your results.* This is no surprise. Caples was a master of "tested advertising methods," and you should become one too. Measure your response rates to see what

elevates and lowers them. Test wording, offers, bonuses, and every other aspect of your promotions. That will tell you what to do to get better results on your next campaign.

There's a wealth of information here from Caples that you can use to create more effective sales materials that yield a greater response. They are all ways to grab and guide your readers' interest and can be used in an endless variety of applications.

Now let's move on to Gary Halbert, who shares additional ways to create more successful promotional campaigns.

HOW TO GET MORE RESPONSE WITHOUT CHANGING YOUR COPY

As you will recall from Chapter 7, when it came to writing effective copy, Gary Halbert recommended going to the source—your best customers—to learn exactly what they were looking for and found appealing in your product. Once you knew that, the sales piece would practically write itself.

Halbert knew there is more to a successful sales piece than just the words. There are many factors that go into grabbing and keeping prospects' attention. There are even some aspects of your interaction with the post office that can affect response. He said that by juggling some of these factors, you can get a better response to your sales piece, even if you don't change one word of the sales letter itself.

The advice from Halbert we'll look at here will be most applicable if you are sending out direct mail sales letters—his methods are very powerful for that purpose. But where it fits, I will point out other possible applications of his ideas in online media as well.

To start with, Halbert offered a number of suggestions designed to make sure your mail is delivered to the post office. He even suggested delivering it there yourself instead of relying on a potentially dishonest letter shop to do it. Halbert also had suggestions on how to make sure the post office delivers your mail, which we can maximize with proper list hygiene and drop-shipping as close as possible to the destination post office. For me, his more interesting suggestions involve techniques that will get prospects to open and then read your mail. Here are some of his best ideas.

Make Your Letters Look More Like First-Class Mail

First-class mail (the method that gives you the fastest delivery at a premium price) gets more attention and respect than third-class mail (now called "Standard" mail and unfortunately often referred to as junk mail). This is not only true for your prospects, but also for the letter shop preparing your mail and the post office itself. So anything you can do to make your sales letter look like a first-class letter will make it more likely that it will be delivered, opened, and read. Here are some ways you can do that.

Use Live Stamps on Your Envelopes Instead of Using a Postage Meter or a Printed Indicia

Even a live bulk stamp gets more respect than printed indicia. Some mailers use antique stamps with attractive pictures. These may require hand-gluing, which makes them more costly to process, but it may be worth it if it gets prospects curious enough to open the envelope.

Place Mailing Addresses on the Envelope with Direct Impression (Heat Transfer, AD MARK, Laser, etc.) Instead of Labels

Labels scream "mailing list" rather than "personal letter." Some marketers are now using handwriting fonts and other methods to really build the impression that the letter is personal.

Don't Put Your Company Name in the Return Address

A return address that says "Ace Plumbing" is obviously an ad, but a classy-looking return address that just gives the street address with no name could be anything. It arouses curiosity.

Don't Put Teaser Copy on the Envelope

Again, teaser copy is a red flag that this is an ad. A plain envelope could be a letter or an invitation—it's all up to the imagination of the prospect. This may be great advice for mailings to new prospects, but be aware of your unique situation. If you are sending a special promotion to your own list—maybe a huge annual sale that your buyers eagerly look forward to—it may in fact be better to put your name and prominent teaser copy on the envelope. As always, test everything for yourself!

Also note that Eugene Schwartz had a different view, advising that we use all the available "real estate" on the envelope. Once again, everything must be tested.

Print the Word "RUSH" in Red on the Envelope

This again arouses curiosity and adds a sense of urgency as well. It adds to the illusion that this is a first-class letter.

Actually Use First-Class Postage

In some cases, Halbert thought it was worthwhile to send sales letters first class (faster delivery at a premium price) rather than third class (Standard mail, which is slower delivery for a lesser cost). Specifically, if the letter weighed less than an ounce, and the unit of sales was more than $39.95, the increased response to first-class postage would outweigh the additional cost. The math may be different today, but the principle is a good one. You'll have to work out the cost-benefit analysis for yourself.

Another advantage of mailing first class is that you get undelivered mail returned to you, which allows you to clean up your mailing list for future campaigns. And there is a psychological factor as well: if your list broker and mail house know you're keeping a "nixie" file (i.e., of returned/undeliverable mail), they will be more likely to give you clean lists and sterling service.

Online Applications

You can adapt these techniques for use in emails as well.

▌ Have it come from an email address that sounds classy.
▌ Use personalization in the subject line and on the email itself, e.g., "Dear Lois"

- ❚ Use a subject line that makes it sound like there is important information in the email.
- ❚ Lead with news in the subject line, especially if you're emailing to your own list.

Make Physical Changes to the Letter

Now that you've made the envelope (or your subject line) more appealing so that prospects will open it, there are things you can do to the letter itself that will make them want to read it. Most of these things can also apply to the layout of your email, web page, or job application.

Make the Letter Easier on the Eyes

There are a number of things you can do to provide "eye relief" so the letter doesn't look so formidable. By setting things up correctly, you can make the letter inviting so that prospects will want to read it. For example:

- ❚ Keep the margins wide and the typeface easy to read.
- ❚ Use lots of subheads that break up the text.
- ❚ Highlight some of the copy by making it bold or another color.
- ❚ Make it look like it would be fun to read, not a slog through a high school textbook.

Camouflage the Sales Material

If prospects open an envelope and immediately see a brochure, they'll know it is a sales letter and have what Halbert called the "Oh Yuck!" reaction. He suggested hiding the brochure in a plain white envelope or not using one at all.

This is something you have to test. (In fact, as I keep saying, you should test everything.) Some mailers have great success with colorful inserts and lift notes. You have to find out what works for you, but Halbert's main point is a great one: don't immediately assault prospects with the fact that this is an ad. Win readers' trust first, and then make the sales pitch.

Add a Photo of the Signer of the Letter

People like to see whom they're dealing with. If they see a picture of the person who is promising to teach them how to make a fortune or train their dog, they feel they have a more personal connection. In any event, in Halbert's experience, this one factor increases response rate. So it's certainly worth a try. For online applications, if you are using HTML format, you can put a photo of the signer above the fold.

Vary Color (or Stock)

If you're including an order card with your direct mail package, print it on yellow stock with black ink. Halbert found this increased response rates because this color combination was easiest to read. He felt it was especially important on order cards that had a lot of copy with small print.

Put Your Phone Number in the Body Copy of Your Letter (or Email, Etc.)

Also invite prospects to call you with any questions. A prominent phone number and invitation to call builds confidence that you are a legitimate business that cares about making your buyers happy. It makes people feel safe, and the safer they feel, the more likely they are to place an order. Halbert suggested you not use an 800 number for this purpose. Again, not everyone agrees on this, so test it for yourself.

Halbert also advised that by taking your own calls instead of using a call service, you can increase orders. Give your dedicated employees the right script, and they will become your best sales staff.

Improve Your Guarantee

Every offer should have a guarantee. This eases prospects' concerns and makes response seem less risky. If you're giving just a 30-day or 60-day guarantee, consider raising it to a full year. Why?

- ▌ It increases response rates.
- ▌ It actually reduces returns. The more time buyers have to put in for a refund, the less likely they are to request one. With a

brief refund period, buyers will hear the clock ticking and will be more likely to ask for a refund if they're not completely satisfied. If they know they have a year to try the product, the urgency isn't there. After a while, they forget that they could get a refund.

Rent a More Responsive Mailing List

This is obvious. Research shows the most important factor in the success of any direct mail or email campaign is the mailing list. If your campaigns are failing, the first thing to do is look at finding a new mailing list. Always keep accurate records of how well or poorly lists do and get rid of the duds.

There's a well-established rule in direct mail marketing called the 40-40-20 rule, which tells us that:

▐ 40 percent of the success of your campaign depends on hitting the right audience with your message (having the right mailing list).

▐ Another 40 percent depends on having an appealing offer that is not only irresistible, but is also time sensitive.

▐ And the last 20 percent depends on the creative elements of your direct mail package.

Personally, I think lists might be more important to your campaign than 40 percent. They may be closer to 60 percent, in my estimation. And please note that when we talk about 40-40-20, this applies to all media, both offline and online.

And There's More . . .

Halbert had other suggestions. For example, some post offices are more efficient than others, so try mailing from several different ones. Also, some letter shops do a better job than others, so test those out as well. Online, some marketers experiment with emailing from multiple IP addresses. I'm pretty sure Halbert would have approved of this approach.

Speaking of testing, Halbert thought it was a good idea to test a small mailing sent first class so you get immediate results about the strength of your sales piece. If you do this before rolling out to a large bulk mailing, you may be able to make quick repairs to a piece that looks like it isn't going to work as well as you hoped.

Isn't that how we do email blasts today? We start by sending out small quantities, see if there are any deliverability issues, and if the early response rate meets our expectations, we email the rest of the list.

There's a lot of information here, and I'm not endorsing all Halbert's suggestions. I do think you should consider them and test them with your own promotional materials and lists.

I really love the idea of finding ways to increase response rates other than changing the basic copy. This is another dimension of successful promotions that deserves attention. By the way, once you've increased your response, you'd better be ready to handle all the orders that start coming in. Visit TheAdvertisingSolution.com and read my article "Don't Drop the Ball."

ALWAYS WORK TO FIND A BETTER WAY

There's no end to the changes we can make in the way we present our message in order to get a better response. Don't ever stop trying something new because you think what you're doing is "good enough." Just one small change could add a huge boost to your ads' effectiveness. You'll never know if you don't put it to the test.

Chapter 9 will go more deeply into the process of testing. It may be a good idea for you to spend some time right now assessing what you've been doing so far to promote yourself. Try to brainstorm some tweaks and changes you could make. Use what you learned in this chapter to get some ideas. You're never stuck with what you've done in the past. Keep forging new trails for increased levels of success.

CHAPTER 9

TEST, TEST, AND TEST AGAIN

THROUGHOUT THIS BOOK I've mentioned in a variety of contexts the importance of testing everything you put out in public. That's the only way you can know your promotions are working, the only way you can make ongoing improvements with confidence, and the only way you can make sure you're getting the best response possible.

If you want to build your business, charitable organization, or image, testing is how you make sure you're going about it the right way. As an example, if you want to build readership of your blog through social media posts or banner ads on other websites, you have to try different methods, compare their results, and see what brings a boost in readership. Here are just some of the questions you might want to ask:

▌ Which headline works best?

- ▋ Does it build response if you include a picture of your product or yourself?
- ▋ Which color gets the most orders or clickthroughs?
- ▋ Does an ad on one website bring a better or worse response than an ad on another website?

It's highly unlikely you will hit on the ideal formula right off the bat based on what you think will work. Without testing, you really have no idea which approach to focus on or which approach will be the best use of your resources.

Our legends spent their entire careers finding the best ways to answer questions like these. So in this chapter I'm going to focus on the process of testing itself and what our legends have to tell us about how you can use testing to increase your level of success.

We'll begin by looking at what John Caples, Claude Hopkins, and David Ogilvy told us about this all-important topic. Then I'll give you some examples of how I've used testing with my own direct marketing clients—sometimes with surprising results—to get the best response rates and build the profitability of their campaigns.

So let's turn first to John Caples, whose book *Tested Advertising Methods* has become a bible for promoters everywhere.

THE VALUE OF TESTING

As we've seen, John Caples' legendary career had its big start in 1926 when he wrote the fabulously successful headline, "They Laughed When I Sat Down at the Piano But When I Started to Play!"

This headline worked so well that it was widely imitated by other advertisers. In fact, it's still being imitated today. As I was writing this, a friend of mine, who is also a copywriter, told me she had just picked up the current issue of *Reader's Digest*, and an eight-page full-color blow-in ad with an attached return envelope—meaning this ad was very expensive—fell out onto the counter. The ad was for a system of products that homeowners can use to plant container gardens. And guess what the headline was?

My neighbors laughed when I ordered,
now they ALL WANT a tomato garden like mine!

Almost a century later, and Caples' groundbreaking headline still works! That's a good sign we should listen to what he has to tell us. So let's start with the process Caples used to determine whether an ad was "successful."

It wasn't deemed successful if he personally liked it or if his client thought it had a nice ring to it. The ad was successful only if it received a tremendous response from buyers, and measuring that response was what John Caples was all about.

Caples was a proponent of measurement in advertising to scientifically prove whether an advertisement worked and to determine which of two different ads worked better. Armed with information like this, it's possible to build increasingly successful campaigns.

He thought it was ridiculous to spend good money on advertising just because you thought the copy was clever, or it looked to you as if it should work. Caples thought those were all just opinions, and opinions that weren't backed up by facts were worthless—and potentially very costly. He believed there was only one way to decide whether to continue to use a specific ad or change it, and that was to measure the number of responses it received, either in terms of inquiries about a product or actual sales.

Caples advocated a three-step approach to creating effective ads:

1. *Capture prospects' attention.* Use headlines, pictures, or whatever it takes to get prospects to notice you.
2. *Maintain prospects' interest.* Make them feel as though they need to keep reading so they will be exposed to the entire message you're trying to convey.
3. *Move prospects to favorable action.* Unless the ad is able to convert interest into action, it is a failure.

Testing is the only certain way to determine whether an ad is doing these three things successfully.

Caples' Special Rule of Testing

Caples went on to outline the following three-step approach to testing the effectiveness of an advertisement. Since he primarily worked in direct mail advertising, he spoke in terms of that medium; however, these principles work across the board, regardless of the type of promotion you're doing.

1. *Accept nothing as true about advertising until you've tested it yourself.* This is the essence of "scientific" advertising. When you first undertake a campaign, you should do some kind of initial testing. Prepare more than one direct mail package, and split test the different versions against one another to see which one does best. The way you do this is to divide your mailing list in half and send a different piece to each half. Then you can collect real data on which piece received a bigger response.

2. *As you test the results of each ad, use what you learn to create an improved version, and then test that.* In this way you build upon your success to create better and better ads (measured, as always, by response rates).

3. *Every new ad is a test of what worked before.* Constantly check results to see the truth of what is working—even if it means admitting you were wrong. Be willing to scrap something you might have loved if something else proves to be better.

The formula Caples suggested was the "LALALAL . . ." rule:

Learn/Adapt/Learn/Adapt/Learn/Adapt/Learn . . .

Following this rule really can pay off. Caples reported a case in which one mail order advertisement sold 19.5 times as much merchandise as another. Without testing, you'd never know by looking at the ads that there would be such an extreme difference between their effectiveness.

Both ads were placed in the same space in the same publication; they were both illustrated with photographs; they had both been written with great care. But one made the right appeal, and the other made the wrong appeal. He didn't say what these appeals were, but perhaps one appealed more to the emotions while the other appealed to the intellect. Both ads looked good, and unless you actually tested the two versions against each other, there would be no way to know which would yield the greater response. Only testing them revealed which ad was built around the better approach.

Caples understood that there may be times when, because of limited budget or because an ad was only going to run once, it might not be possible to pretest. In that case, he suggested it would be a good idea to learn from other advertisers who had tested different aspects of ads and apply their findings to your own ads. In his books, Caples was glad to help other writers by presenting the rules he'd developed over time, such as important elements in headlines that could be used by any ad writer.

We'll be looking more deeply into the specific methods Caples used to test his ads later in this chapter. First I want to step back in time and look at what Claude Hopkins had to share about applying scientific testing to promotions.

GETTING IT DOWN TO A SCIENCE

As you will recall, Claude Hopkins published his book *Scientific Advertising* back in 1923, making him one of the pioneers in this field. Hopkins said all forms of advertising really boil down to one thing: salesmanship. Salesmanship is something that can and should be measured.

If a company had a team of salesmen, they wouldn't just send them out and then accept without question whatever results each salesman turned in. They would measure and compare all their results to see who was doing the best job. The salesmen with the best results would be promoted, while the worst ones would be trained on the techniques the best ones used. If they still couldn't measure up, they would be advised to take up another profession.

It should be the same with each piece of advertising.

For each of his ads, Hopkins kept track of the cost per customer and the cost per sale. These are measurements we take for granted today, but in his day, this approach was revolutionary. Hopkins used these measurements as the yardsticks by which he compared the results of different ads, so he could fine-tune his methods with each campaign. Then he turned his findings into principles that he applied and tested in campaigns for other products.

The next generation of advertisers placed a high value on Hopkins' contributions to the field. One of our other legends, David Ogilvy, said, "Nobody should be allowed to have anything to do with advertising until he has read this book [*Scientific Advertising*] seven times. It changed the course of my life."

The Secret of Success: Learn from Your Mistakes

How was Hopkins able to create so many successful advertising campaigns for his clients? It was the result of hard work. Hopkins attributed his success to the fact that he made a great number of small mistakes, and he learned from every one of them. As a result, he claimed never to have repeated a mistake. Along the way, he came up with some great advertising principles that have endured through the years. But it was the tedious making of small mistakes and learning from them that was the foundation of his achievements in the field.

This is reminiscent of the famous story about the great inventor Thomas Edison. After Edison had failed thousands of times in his quest to develop a nickel-iron battery, an associate asked him if he wasn't disappointed about not getting any results after so long. Edison replied:

Results! Why, man, I have gotten a lot of results! I know several thousand things that won't work.

He wasn't daunted. With each "failure," he saw himself as farther along the path to ultimate victory. And he finally did prevail, patenting his battery in 1901.

Hopkins said no one can depend on his personal judgment or experience to determine the right way to advertise a product.

In advertising, many factors we don't understand come into play. That's why it's so important to test, correct, test, and correct. This is what Hopkins meant by "scientific advertising": advertising built upon fixed principles and carried out according to fundamental laws. The copywriter has an obligation to be guided by actual data in developing campaigns. Without that, the client is most likely be throwing money away.

Another favorite Hopkins principle is that he directed all his campaigns to an individual member of his target audience. He did not consult with managers or boards of directors on the best way to advertise their product—he felt their viewpoints were distorted. Instead, he submitted his ideas (by which he meant he tested them) to the ". . . simple folks around me who typify America."

They were the customers he was trying to engage. Their behavior would make or break a campaign, and therefore, "Their reactions are the only ones that count."

Today's most successful promoters know this. Surveying your top customers is often the best way to find out what they want.

Hopkins was not impressed by "theories of advertising" that were not proved with hard data. He thought most of these were based on exceptional cases and limited experience. Theories that are based on chance or imagination are likely to mislead other advertisers who try to follow them.

Hopkins mostly worked on ads in publications. It can be difficult to get exact measurements from ads in this medium because it is not always possible to determine the response that comes directly from the ad itself. He also worked on mail order (direct mail) advertising, which he said gave the most precise data about what worked in an ad and what didn't.

The Sale Is in the Details

When it comes to writing ads or sales pieces (all of which would then be subjected to the strictest testing), Hopkins believed it is important for the ad writer to have detailed and full knowledge of the product he is writing about. His research showed again and again that the more reasons an ad presented for why the prospect should obey the call to action, the more likely it was the prospect would follow through.

A great example of this was a campaign he developed for a new product, Palmolive Shaving Cream. Hopkins knew men tended to be loyal to whatever brand they used regularly, and the challenge was to win them away to a new brand. But at the time, no one knew what men wanted in a shaving cream, so there was no basis upon which to build an ad. Research was required.

Hopkins sent out a team of researchers to interview hundreds of men and find out which specific features they most valued in a shaving cream. Then he took his findings to Palmolive's chief chemist and said: "This is what men want. What can you tell me about Palmolive Shaving Cream that specifically answers each of these desires?" It didn't matter that competing shaving creams probably used similar ingredients and offered the same features. Palmolive would be the first to address these issues in an ad, and so would seem to be unique in offering these benefits. Hopkins incorporated what he learned in his ad, and sales surged. As Hopkins said:

> We were the first to give figures on results. And one actual figure counts for more than countless platitudes.

Hopkins did the required work so he could substitute "actual figures for atmospheric claims." As a result, within 18 months, Palmolive Shaving Cream dominated the market.

Some Things Never Change

Even back in Hopkins' time, people were saying the world was changing and that advertising had to come up with new ideas. Hopkins acknowledged that fads and fancies come and go, styles of advertising vary, and new campaigns require new keynotes (what Ogilvy called "big ideas"). Ads that just imitated other ads that were already stale would not succeed. "But," he said, "human nature does not change." He stated that the principles he set down in his book "are as enduring as the Alps."

Hopkins also acknowledged that advertising was getting more expensive, and therefore posed more of a risk to the advertiser. In addition, the competition was much stiffer. This was no reason to despair. It just meant there was an even greater need for the benefits of scientific advertising.

Reading Hopkins' ads today, we may find them quaint. That's understandable. Many of them were written in the 1910s and 1920s. Products were different then and seem terribly old-fashioned to people today. Even the words and expressions people used back then were different. But the principles Hopkins used to write those ads are the same ones used today to make ads for smartphones and microwavable dinners. In our multibillion-dollar world of advertising, Hopkins' principles of scientific advertising still rule.

Regardless of what you're promoting today, be prepared to test everything you send out. Keep track of your results so you can determine which of your "salesmen" are doing the best job of influencing prospects to buy. Just as Hopkins did with Palmolive Shaving Cream, do your research to find out what your target audience is looking for in your product. Then build your promotional materials around those features, showing how the product you offer meets all those desires. And continue testing.

It may seem like a lot of work, but it will pay off in the end with more sales—whatever a sale means to you, whether it's more bodies in your store, more clicks on your website, more likes on your Facebook page, or a promotion at work!

18 MIRACLES OF RESEARCH

Legend David Ogilvy always stressed the importance of working hard to get the information needed to create a really great ad, one that did its job of persuading people to buy. In line with the theme of this chapter, Ogilvy's key to creating such an ad was research. He once wrote:

> *Advertising people who ignore research are as dangerous as generals who ignore decodes of enemy signals.*

Of course, ad writers also need creativity (Ogilvy himself was one of the industry's most creative copywriters), but without the research to back them up, their copy just would not have the ammunition to be convincing.

Ogilvy offered a list of 18 benefits that this kind of investigation offered advertisers. He called them "Miracles of Research." Let's briefly look at these 18 benefits:

1. *Research will confirm your reputation.* Research can tell you where your company stands by measuring its reputation among various communities: consumers, journalists, academia, the government, etc. Through polling and interviews, you can learn exactly what these people think of you. If you discover that a bad reputation is indeed interfering with your company's growth, you would now know exactly where the problems lie, and what you need to do to polish your image.

2. *Research will force you to do your math.* By applying mathematical models to the responses you get to tests of a new product you're about to release, you can predict sales. That can help you decide how much you can comfortably afford to spend to advertise the product, based on your expected profits. If the cost of advertising isn't justified by the potential profits, you might want to rethink your plans. Ogilvy reported research indicating 60 percent of new products fail in test markets. Wouldn't it be better to know your product's chances of success through testing before rolling out an expensive campaign?

3. *Research will tell you if this is a good or bad product before you launch.* Research can measure consumer responses to new products while they are still in the conceptual stage. Are people even going to be interested in the product you plan to produce? It would be best to find out early in the process. This can save you a bundle if it keeps you from wasting money developing and advertising a product that no one will want to buy.

4. *Research will help you compare yourself to your competition.* By testing a new product you plan to develop against one your competition is already selling, you can see whether your version will be able to match the popularity of your competitor's product. You will also learn what you need to do to make your version more attractive.

5. *Research will eliminate guessing.* You won't have to guess at what your prospects want. You can test different formulations, flavors, or fragrances ahead of time to determine which version of your product will be most appealing to your target customer. This will help set you up for success from the outset.

6. *Research will lead you to the best design.* Package design plays a big role in the success of products. For example, the color of a package or the font used in a product name can make a huge difference in how appealing it is to potential buyers. Research can help you determine which design will get the most favorable attention and motivate people to buy.

7. *Research will create your positioning.* You can use research to determine how best to position your product. Maybe you've created a new snack food. Will you get the most sales by offering it as a yummy treat or a healthy one? Testing will help you discover which approach will appeal to the biggest audience.

8. *Research will determine your target audience.* Do you know who will actually want to buy your product? You would do well to determine your target audience before rolling out a big campaign. For example, you may think your product will appeal to 20-somethings and plan to advertise to that demographic, when in fact you should be targeting 40-somethings. Research could keep you from making a costly mistake.

9. *Research will uncover what consumers really want to know or have you talk about.* What kinds of variables do buyers focus on when they think about your product? What lan-

guage do they use to describe it? For example, do they select a type of soap primarily for its cleansing properties or its beauty properties? The answer will determine which benefits you should stress in your advertising. Your research will help you identify the important variables.

10. *Research will create your umbrella brand.* Once you have a successful product with an established name, you can use that name to sell related products. But which ones? Ogilvy gave the example of Lever Brothers, who wanted to extend the success of their Dove brand, but weren't sure what kind of product would be the best fit. They did some consumer research that showed they would have a winning product by placing the Dove name on dishwashing liquid.

11. *Research will keep you moving forward.* Never rest on your laurels. You may have a successful product, but you must keep checking to see if consumers continue to see your product as desirable—and that requires research. If your image is slipping, you need to know about it. Ogilvy said that in many cases, this happens when consumers notice you're using cheaper ingredients. So before you start making major changes to your formula, do research to find out whether it's noticeable, and if your customers find it objectionable.

12. *Research will enable you to get the jump on your competition.* Ogilvy suggested using research to check up on what your competitors are doing. They must be doing their own research, so what do their test markets tell them? What are their profit margins, and how do yours compare? How much are they paying for raw materials, as opposed to what you're paying? Who are their suppliers? Ogilvy claimed the information is out there if you know how to look for it.

13. *Research will shine a light on your best benefit(s).* Every great ad contains a promise. Ogilvy quoted the words of Samuel Johnson from 1759:

> *Promise, large Promise is the soul of an Advertisement.*

But have people today learned this critical lesson? No, they haven't, said Ogilvy:

Advertising which promises no benefit to the consumer does not sell, yet the majority of campaigns contain no promise whatever. (That is the most important sentence in this book. Read it again.)

Ogilvy reported research showing that advertisements using headlines that promise a benefit are read by four times more people than advertisements without such headlines. Even so, many advertisers fail to put a promise in the headline. Don't just give information in a headline; give a benefit. Don't just say "One-Hour Dry Cleaning Service." Say "Get Ready on Short Notice with Our One-Hour Dry Cleaning Service." Or "Our One-Hour Dry Cleaning Service Makes You Look Like a Million Bucks."

Determining the best promise for an ad, said Ogilvy, is the most valuable contribution research can make to the ad creation process. Using split-run testing is a great way to see which promise works best. A promise that is both persuasive and unique will be the most powerful, but don't try to guess. To prove that your promise is doing the job, you need data to back you up.

14. *Research will identify your best bonus.* An important part of many ads is the "premium" offered—some kind of free gift or bonus. Some free gifts will be more appealing than others, and some will be of no interest to your target audience. Research will show you which premium will get you the biggest response.

15. *Research will ensure you are being understood properly.* We all interpret things differently, and it's critical that you know how your target audience is interpreting your ad. You may think you know what your ad is saying, but your prospect may not read it the way you do. You may think you're being funny, but your prospect may think you're being disrespectful

or annoying. You may think your ad for a financial course is describing a great new way to make money, but your prospect may think it sounds like a lot of work. Only by testing your advertising will you know if it's conveying the right message.

16. *Research will tell you if you have converted buyers from the competition.* Ogilvy talked about pretesting television commercials, and his findings here are applicable to any kind of promotion you may be doing. He said testing recall of commercials has no relation to their success at getting consumers to buy the product. The more important issue to test is a change in brand preferences. Has your target audience actually been converted away from your competitor in favor of your product?

    He also said to keep testing ads for "wear-out." Eventually, even the best ad will lose its power because people's values change over time. Even if your ad is working, keep testing to see if its numbers continue to hold up. As soon as they start slipping, be ready with the next big campaign idea (that hopefully you've also been pretesting all along).

17. *Research will tell you if they are reading and remembering.* Despite point 16 above (that recall doesn't equate to buying), if people don't read or remember ads at all, they can't be persuaded by them to take action. Research can tell you whether people are reading and remembering your ads.

18. *And research can (and will) settle arguments.* I love this last point. I can just see Ogilvy sitting at a boardroom table with a recalcitrant client and pulling out a professional-looking research report to prove that his advice about an ad is better than the idiotic opinion of his know-nothing client. But I may have seen too many episodes of *Mad Men.*

    Anyway, there are bound to be disagreements as people consider different aspects of an ad. Having research available can help you make the best decisions possible, backed by science.

Marketing is a difficult field. Being successful at it doesn't come from making decisions based on opinions or feelings. To get people to buy your product, you have to know what they're thinking, what they like, and what you have to do to get their interest, overcome their skepticism, and win their hearts. The only way to know these things for sure is by doing the research.

So keep Ogilvy's list handy, and look to it for inspiration whenever you wonder if it's really worth the effort to do what I'm urging you to do: test, test, and test every aspect of your promotional campaigns. It might help you create your own marketing "miracle."

SURPRISING WAYS TO TEST YOUR ADVERTISING

Now let's return to that avid copy tester John Caples. Here is one bit of Caples' wisdom that tells the whole story:

> *Test everything. Doubt everything. Be interested in theories, but don't spend a large sum of money on a theory without spending a little money to test it first.*

Caples and his team spent millions of dollars to learn the answers to questions like:

> *What kind of headlines attract the most readers?*
>
> *What kind of copy will be most successful in persuading people to buy your product or service?*

They spent millions, but used their findings to make many more millions. In spite of Caples' success, however, he knew there was no end to the discoveries that could be made. He encouraged the next generations of copywriters and ad makers to come up with new questions and new sales appeals. But how would these ad creators know which of their new ideas were the most effective? They would test, of course, to make sure advertising dollars were spent where they would bring the best results.

In his classic book *Tested Advertising Methods*, Caples offered many ways to put an ad to the test. These techniques ran the gamut from simple to complex, and the test you would choose would depend on the type of issue you were looking at and how much time and money you had to throw at the problem. You might be surprised to see some of the methods Caples suggested. Here are a few of the techniques that are most applicable to what you're doing in your marketing today:

∎ *Put your newly written ad aside until the next day.* As a copywriter, your first and best line of defense is yourself. There are different stages of creating an ad. First, there's the stage where you're full of enthusiasm, dashing off your brilliant ideas. But when you look at what you've written again the next day, you're a different person—cool and objective. Thank goodness.

Now you can see where your language can be simplified, where you're missing a clear call to action, where you can bring in the reader more quickly by deleting that opening paragraph you were so in love with the day before. Always look at everything again the next day. With clearer eyes and a broader perspective, you will find many things that need to be fixed and improved.

∎ *Ask somebody to read your ad copy aloud to you.* Does this sound strange? Maybe you're thinking, shouldn't you read your copy aloud to someone else? But Caples explained the problem with reading your copy to someone else is that you know your own copy, so you read it with the right emphasis— and you learn nothing from the process.

When someone else reads your copy out loud to you—cold, unfamiliar with the material—you can tell right away where the stumbling blocks are, where the person obviously misunderstands your unclear copy, and where sentences are awkward or too long.

Now use what you learn. If the person doesn't understand something, that means your target audience probably won't understand it either. So look at how you can change the copy. If the person stumbles over your wording, smooth it out. This is a very effective way to perfect a piece.

▐ *Opinion test by interview.* Now that you've perfected your ad to some degree, get other people's opinions of it. Caples suggested using actual prospects for the product. For example, show ads for dog food to dog owners.

Always give people a choice of which ad, headline, illustration, etc., they prefer. If you just show them your ad and ask them whether they like it, they'll probably say yes because they don't want to hurt your feelings. But if you show them two headlines and ask which one they like better, you'll get a more honest opinion.

However, be aware that opinion tests by themselves are not enough; they are only opinions. Caples said you should always back up opinion tests with sales tests.

▐ *Sales tests.* Caples offered a number of different types of sales tests, including looking at responses to mail order tests, testing the use of coupons, testing the value of following up coupons with calls by a sales representative, offering samples and free literature, using coupons vs. "hidden offers" that were described in the text but not made obvious by the addition of a coupon, and split testing. By testing selected variables in ads against one another and measuring which produced the greater response, Caples developed a scientific approach to creating effective ads.

Caples acknowledged that advertising could never be an exact science like chemistry. In a chemistry lab, you can have complete control over all the variables. But in advertising, there are too many unknown variables, and they are always changing. For example, the news of the day could be bad and cast a shadow on every ad published on that particular day. You would never be able to anticipate that through pretesting.

That doesn't mean there aren't great advantages to running tests. You may never be able to predict with precision how an ad will do, but you can quickly identify ads that don't work at all, compared to ads that work very well. And then you can keep improving on the ads that work well, to make them work even better.

As Caples said, an automobile manufacturer would never buy a trainload of axles or seat fabric without running many pretests to ensure the money was well spent. Why would he buy trainloads of advertising with nothing more to go on than his personal opinion? Advertising would never live up to its full potential to benefit business until testing was made part of the process.

Finally, let's look at Caples' "one rule that never changes":

Test everything on a small scale before you spend money on a large scale. Testing enables you to keep your finger on the public pulse. It enables you to sense trends in advance. It enables you to separate the wheat from the chaff, the sheep from the goats, the winning ideas from the duds. It enables you to multiply the results you get from the dollars you spend in advertising.

SOME OF MY OWN "MIRACLES OF RESEARCH"

Over the years, I've run numerous tests on sales pieces I've developed for clients. These were primarily tests of direct mail sales pieces. As I keep saying, anything that holds true for one form of advertising or promotion holds true for all forms. So even if you're trying to get subscribers to your blog or are preparing a job application, you have to determine what works best for you to get the results you want.

I'm going to present you with four examples of tests I've run for clients in an attempt to get an increasingly better response. They show how testing even small variables can make a huge difference in the number of responses an ad produces.

The Power of an Image

I started out my career in the marketing department of a financial publisher. The founder was a commodity trader who put together a series of home study courses that gave average individuals information and tools they could use to learn how to trade commodities themselves.

All our advertising was built around the founder's image. His message was that he started with no money and very little education, but learned how to trade and made his fortune as a result. He assured prospects that anyone could use the courses he developed to learn how to trade as well. His picture was prominent in all the sales pieces, and it was important that we used the most appealing image—one that portrayed the kind of character people most trusted and could identify with.

We tested all kinds of images—the founder in a cowboy hat, a baseball cap, or no hat; in a denim shirt, a business suit, or a leather jacket. And we tested every combination of hat and clothing. We found very conclusively that the combination that brought the largest, most reliable response was the denim shirt and cowboy hat. Once we determined that, we used that image in all our advertising, with spectacular results. Without the testing, we never would have known which combination worked best and might have used a less appealing image.

The More You Tell, the More You Sell

One of my clients had been sending out a 36-page sales letter. The length itself did not seem problematic. I've sent out many sales pieces that were even longer with great results. But this particular piece was cumbersome and poorly written. It was a bear to get through because it was extremely repetitive. Reading it, you felt as though you were slogging through tons of excess information just to get to the main point.

So we decided to trim the letter to a nice, snappy 24 pages. The copy was made tighter and more concise. The numerous repetitions were removed, and as a result, the whole piece flowed better. We couldn't wait to run our tests.

But to our surprise, even though the 24-page piece seemed so much better written and more interesting to read, the original 36-page piece had double the response rate!

One of my favorite marketing principles is: "The more you tell, the more you sell." Well, it's still true. Plus, you have to consider the target audience. Perhaps for this particular product, the most likely buyers actually liked the rambling, homespun feel of the original piece. In any case, we kept using it and continued to get a great response.

Paying More/Paying Out

In general, we find that putting a live stamp on an envelope, as opposed to printed indicia, increases response rates. There are probably a number of factors involved, but a big one is that people are more likely to open an envelope with a live stamp. Printed indicia is a dead giveaway that there's an ad or a bill inside the envelope. But the live stamp makes recipients think there could be something more important inside. Of course, once the envelope is open, a brilliant headline will hopefully tempt the prospect to read further.

But what about when you're sending a postcard? All the copy on the postcard is right out there in the open, and the prospect can see immediately that it is an ad. You would think it wouldn't matter if you use live stamps or indicia. Since I'm always looking to save my clients' money—and it's much more labor intensive and therefore expensive to attach live stamps—I was hoping that using indicia would not affect the response negatively. But I wanted to know for sure, so I ran a test for one of my clients who sold training courses to insurance salesmen. In fact, I ran more than a dozen tests and mailed more than 150,000 pieces for that test.

And every single time, the live stamp drew a bigger response. That wasn't what I was hoping to find and it didn't make any sense to me, but I was glad to know the truth. It proves you should never assume you know the answer and should always put it to the test.

Size Matters

As a final example of my own research, I'll tell you what careful testing showed me about the size of a direct-mail package. Two commonly used envelope sizes are 6 by 9 and 9 by 12. The 6-by-9 envelope costs considerably less to print and mail. Using a 9-by-12 envelope bumps you up to the next postage class, making it more expensive to mail. With a mailing of perhaps hundreds of thousands of pieces, that could mean many thousands of dollars in extra postage. That's not a problem if the response rate increases in turn, so the additional profits offset the additional postage expense. But how will you know?

By testing, of course.

I ran three separate tests of this issue for clients and found that in every case, the 9-by-12 envelope worked significantly better—so much so that the increased production and postage costs were completely offset, and a much greater profit was realized overall.

But again, without testing you would never know this.

For these particular mailing pieces for this product, if my client had cut corners by using the smaller envelope, it would have decreased profits. However, for your product, there might be a different result. You can't make decisions for yourself based on other people's research. You have to determine through testing what works best for you.

THESE PRINCIPLES WORK FOR EVERY MEDIUM

Many of the examples used throughout this chapter have focused on direct mail. That's because our legends did a lot of their research in this area. Several of them even commented that direct mail campaigns, where you send out thousands of pieces at a time, are ideal for performing split-run tests.

However, I want to emphasize that the need for and benefits of testing everything you do apply to every medium.

▐ If you own a store and are placing an ad in the newspaper, talk to the publisher about doing split-run testing. That means you create two different ads—maybe one with a "Buy one, get one 50 percent off" offer and another for "25 percent off." Tell readers to bring in the ad to get the discount. The newspaper will run half its copies with one ad, and the other half with the other. Then you can count how many ads of each type are turned over to you, and you'll know which offer works better for future promotions.

▍ You can do something similar with banner ads if you're advertising online. The site you're advertising on can alternate two different ads, and you can count and compare the number of clickthroughs to your site.

▍ If you want to make sure you're advertising on the best site, you can run the same ad on two different sites and see which brings the most clicks.

▍ You can use split-run principles to test your email advertising just as you would for a direct mail campaign.

▍ Do you wonder which of your blog entries are likely to get the most attention? Run different titles and see which ones get the most readership, Facebook likes, and new subscribers. Use what you learn to write on topics your readers are most interested in.

These are just a few suggestions. The possibilities are endless. I just want you to understand that human psychology is complex, and we cannot always predict what will work best based on our own personal preferences or opinions. Start thinking about how you can test your promotions, and then adapt what you do based on the results. Take this scientific approach, and you will find yourself getting a better and better response every time.

CHAPTER 10

THE TOP TEN LESSONS FROM THE LEGENDS

D O YOU HAVE A MESSAGE YOU want to get out into the world? Maybe you want to tell people about a product or service you are trying to sell. Maybe you are associated with a nonprofit group, and you want to raise funds or just build awareness by telling people about the important work you're doing. Maybe you want to find a job and need to know the best way to market yourself. Maybe you're trying to establish yourself as a blogger or a YouTube personality.

No matter what your message is and what platform you're using to broadcast it, there are basic principles of promotion you can use to make sure you're working as effectively as possible to spread the word.

These principles for the most part boil down to one thing: human psychology.

Human psychology has not changed over the millennia. These rules for reaching and influencing others have been used by promoters for centuries, but they were laid out for us with great clarity by a group of admen who developed their craft during the 20th century, and whom we call our legends.

Throughout this book, you have read about the discoveries of these master promoters, and learned how you can apply them to your own fields of endeavor. We've covered a broad territory, and I thought it would be helpful to use this last chapter to look at some of the main principles—the lessons from our legends—and give you some more ideas about how you can adapt them for your own use.

From all my reading and extensive research on our six legends, I have arrived at these ten overriding lessons for putting together a promotional campaign that produces the best results. I think all six would agree on these.

LESSON 1: KNOW YOUR PRODUCT

In order to sell something, you need to develop some kind of description of what you're offering that you can present to prospects. For the sake of simplicity, we'll call it a sales letter, although it could be web copy, a job application, a speech—really, we're talking about any form of communication.

Once you've decided what you're selling and what medium you will use to sell it, the next step is to come up with the words that will convey your message. This is what we refer to as the creative process, and it can be a little daunting, especially if you've never done anything like this before.

Many would-be promoters make the mistake of sitting down before a blank sheet of paper or computer screen and waiting for inspiration to come to them. But all our legends tell us that's not the way to create great copy. What you end up with—assuming you get anything down at all—is nothing more than a set of ideas with no real basis. It's imagination with no meat to it. Plus, it's hard to come up with ideas out of nowhere. So you often end up sitting there for hours, completely blank, as your frustration builds, along with a growing dread that you'll never come up with anything at all.

And that's a shame because it doesn't have to be that hard.

Everything you need to get started and see you through the entire process is right before you. The sales pitch you're struggling to come up with is within the product itself and the information you have about it.

The task you face is more a matter of doing your research and organizing what you find than trying to create something new out of your own head. All the legends spoke of this, but just to give two examples:

▌ *David Ogilvy* pored over technical reports from the manu-facturing department to arrive at the perfect headline for his Rolls-Royce ad. The line was actually written by a technician. Ogilvy just needed a brilliant eye to recognize pay dirt when he saw it.

▌ *Eugene Schwartz* mined gold from the books he sold for Rodale by sifting through the manuscript for selling points. Once he'd pulled out and organized the key information, the sales piece practically wrote itself.

So how can you apply this method for yourself?

No matter what you're selling, you start by gathering all the information you have about it. Stay relaxed during this process. Don't get anxious. You're just putting together everything you know about your product. There's no need to get tied up in knots about it.

If you're selling an actual product, get all the details on how it's made, what it does, how it's an improvement over the competition, and any special effort that's put into creating it. You especially want information about unique or quality features. These will form the basis of the smaller headlines and subheads in your final piece. What is the chief benefit it offers? This might end up being your main headline, but don't worry about that yet. Just get the information, and spend some time studying it to see what jumps out at you.

The process is the same no matter what the product is—or even if you're not selling a product but writing a letter to raise support for a nonprofit organization. If your product is yourself (say, a job application or a profile for a dating site), do the same thing. Make a list of everything you can think of about yourself that might be relevant, and your responses to the different questions you must answer will naturally begin to fall into place.

Trying to write something with no idea where to begin is extremely difficult. Start by finding out everything you can about your product, and the ideas and connections will soon start to take shape.

LESSON 2: KNOW YOUR AUDIENCE

Another aspect of crafting a successful message is to specifically gear it to the desires, needs, interests, and language of the people you're trying to sell to. If your best prospects are teenage boys with an interest in skateboarding and hip-hop, you will present your message very differently than if your best prospects are conservative, middle-aged men. What works well for selling to one group will fail miserably at appealing to the other.

If your best prospects are just like you, then you have a good head start, because you know yourself. But even then, you should never assume that you know *everything* about what other people want. To get the best results, you have to make the effort to find out.

Our legends told us again and again that you have to get out among the people you want to sell to. You should also spend some time immersing yourself in the culture they live in. Go to the movies they attend. Read their most popular magazines. Listen to them talk in elevators, in restaurants, at ball games, or wherever your prospects tend to hang out.

If you've got the means, you might consider asking them about themselves. Send out questionnaires to lists of people who are like your prospects or interview them personally. Speaking of lists, if you have a list of likely prospects, you can learn a lot about them by taking that list to a company that does "list modeling." There are a number of data companies that have scads of information on huge numbers of individuals, including Epsilon Targeting, Experian, and Equifax, among others.

These companies have access to a surprising array of information. For example, Epsilon Targeting owns North America's largest survey response database, covering more than 35 million households and 65 million individuals. It holds information on 1,000 data points, including attitudinal and behavioral measures. Chances are, you are in one or more of these databases as well.

What do they do to get all this information on us? The fact is that we provide it ourselves. A lot of it comes from places like warranty cards and surveys that people fill out without even thinking about it, which is then compiled by a large number of consumer and business data cooperatives.

All that information is sold to or shared with companies like Epsilon Targeting and Equifax, which enter it into their pool of data to be sorted into large numbers of categories and analyzed as needed.

OK, so there you are with your own list of maybe 10,000 people who bought your product, made inquiries, made donations, and so on. You don't know anything else about them, but you want to know more so you can create more successful promotions.

You can send your 10,000 names to one of these huge data companies—let's say Epsilon Targeting. They run your list against their file of maybe 30 million names to see how many are in their larger database. Maybe they find 5,000 matches. And while you don't know anything about these 5,000 people, Epsilon Targeting knows a lot, like their average age and income, how large their families are, what kind of home they live in, their hobbies, and maybe even their health problems. As a result, you can get a pretty good picture of what your buyers look like.

Now you can picture your average buyer in your mind. Are most of them dog owners? You can use some kind of dog imagery in your examples. Are they active sportsmen and women? That gives you more ideas on how to appeal to them. Are they predominantly single? That's also important information.

What if you're just starting out and don't have a list of your own? Consult with a list broker (someone who sells mailing lists). The broker will have lists of people who bought products like yours and can tell you their characteristics.

All this gives you a much clearer idea of whom you're selling to and how to speak their language, capture and hold their interest, and influence their choices and behavior.

LESSON 3: GET STARTED

Coming up with promotional materials isn't always easy, and it doesn't get any easier by staring at a blank page for hours. You just have to get started.

If you're having difficulty, it would be an excellent idea to look back at Chapter 7 for the method Eugene Schwartz used. His approach is a great way to get over any initial hesitation. To quickly summarize how you can apply his method, first input all the information you have into your computer. Then read it over and over. Sift through it. Move pieces around. See what pops out at you as a possible headline or subhead. Don't try to come up with something new. Just reorganize what you have and see what it's telling you.

Not only will this help you see a piece begin to take shape, but a marvelous thing will happen as well. The more time you spend going over the material, the more your subconscious mind will start going to work on it for you, coming up with new connections on its own. These new connections will start popping into your mind while you're preparing dinner, brushing your teeth, or raking leaves. Write them down as they come to you and then add them to the document you've already started on your computer.

Little by little, your marketing piece (sales piece, letter, web page, blog intro, whatever) will begin to form into a structure. Now comes the fun part (it's fun if you're a writer, or at least a budding writer, but it can be interesting even if you're not). Now you can start refining—perfecting sentences, changing the language to best appeal to your target audience, filling in examples or anecdotes, and so on.

You'll be amazed at how you can begin creating the promotional material you want, but it will never happen if you don't get started. So use these simple ideas to get things going, and see what develops.

LESSON 4: MAKE SURE YOU GET EVERY PART OF THE PACKAGE RIGHT

Every promotional package is made up of a number of different parts. Each of them serves a different purpose and is essential to the overall success of the campaign. If you're writing a sales letter, a web page, a blog, or an ad in a publication, you should have a headline that captures attention and gets people wanting to read more. That should be followed by copy that further presents your case and convinces readers they need and should get what you're selling.

If you expect people to give you money, or even their email address, you should offer some sort of guarantee. It could be a money-back guarantee or an assurance that you will not sell their email address to another company, depending on what you are expecting them to give you. The purpose of the guarantee is to make prospects more comfortable about risking their money or personal information. Without it, people are less likely to comply.

Then you'll need an order page or order form where you'll put in more sales copy and provide a way for people to give you the information you need to complete the deal. The order form should be clear and easy to use, or you may lose people at the end. For online applications, the "abandoned shopping cart" is partly the result of an order area that is not user-friendly.

You might also include testimonials from other satisfied customers. Especially in this day of social media, we look to others to confirm our decisions. Testimonials can be very powerful.

Also, depending on your medium, you may have other elements included in your package. Sidebars are very popular. These are sections of interesting or important information that don't flow with the body text, but are pulled out into a box where they make a very specific point. They may provide a bulleted list of advantages, a list of ingredients, a personal message from you, or whatever you want that will have more impact if it's separated from the rest of the text, where it is more likely to be noticed.

You might also want a FAQ area, special instructions, news items, inspirational quotes from famous people, photographs, cartoons, charts and tables . . . really, there's no limit on what you can include in your promotional package, as long as it supports your sales message and keeps people reading.

If you have a printed piece to mail out, you might include a lift note (like a sidebar, but printed separately from the main piece) or a return envelope. Your outside envelope can have copy that entices people to look inside, or it can have no copy, which is mysterious and can also get people to look inside. You have to find out what works best for you.

If you have a website, you have lots of space for additional information, such as "About Us" or "Press Room" pages and videos.

The bottom line is, you need to consider your whole campaign and what elements will be included in it. Then think about the special benefit each part will add to the overall package, and how you can maximize its impact. Don't forget to add sales copy to the order form. Make sure your headline is intriguing and informative and gets people to keep reading. Don't fail to place a prominent call to action. If you add a sidebar, make sure it's relevant and doesn't contain extraneous information that sends people off to another website. Be certain that each part of your campaign pulls its weight and strengthens your message.

LESSON 5: IT'S ALL ABOUT THE PROSPECT

Of course you are interested in your product and in convincing your prospects. But what are your prospects interested in?

Themselves and what they want.

That means that to be successful, you must be very interested in those things too.

The purpose of your promotional copy is not to build yourself up or impress people with your vast vocabulary. The purpose is to pull prospects in. While you want to get them interested in you and what you offer, the way to do that is to make your campaign about them. Of course, this doesn't mean you won't be talking about yourself and your product, but you should do it in a way that keeps the prospect's desires and needs in the forefront. Your copy has to address what the prospect cares about, and how your product will fulfill those needs.

And always remember that you are speaking to one person, not to a crowd, even if you are mailing out a million sales pieces or your website is getting a million hits. Each prospect is looking at your material alone. Each one wants to feel as though he or she is being seen as an individual and will be treated that way. Through your copy, you want to be in a conversation with one prospect and you want the prospect to feel that way as well.

So write to one person in language that will make that person feel understood and valued. Make it clear what you will do for him or her. Include the benefits so readers will see exactly what you can offer them—as individuals—that will make their lives better, easier, and more enjoyable. For example, you may think that the important message about the new juicer you created is its sophisticated engine design, its improved torque ratio, and how thoroughly it breaks through the cell wall of fruits and vegetables—and you should certainly mention all this in your copy. When you do, however, explain why this is important to your readers. Stress that with this machine, juicing is fast, cleanup is easy, and drinking the juice will have them glowing with health.

Put yourself in your readers' place. What would you want to know about the product that would persuade you to buy it? That's what your readers need to have explained to them, as appealingly as possible. Your readers and their interests should be at the center of everything you write. It can take a little finesse, but basically you want to talk about your product or service while keeping that one reader as your focal point.

If you maintain the proper balance, you will be able to get in all the important information about the product while personally engaging your readers and making them understand how important it is to acquire what you're offering.

LESSON 6: BE PASSIONATE ABOUT WHAT YOU'RE SELLING

One of my favorite stories in this book is the one legend Robert Collier told about how when he was a young man working in a coal company, he had a great idea for how to sell their coal to utility companies. It had to do with some special property of the coal that made it uniquely suited for a certain use. Based on that "aha" moment, Collier, with no experience as a copywriter, sat down and wrote such a powerful sales piece that it made a fortune for the company he worked for. Utility companies couldn't wait to get their hands on the product.

What was it that gave that piece so much power? Collier said it himself:

I was full of an idea, and it bubbled out all over the letter. And that is what counts.

If you are distant and cool about what you're trying to sell, you're not going to be able to build much warmth in your prospects. A wet match lights no fires. But enthusiasm is contagious—and it sells. Even if you are not the most polished writer, if you love what you're writing about and really believe in its ability to make people's lives better and more enjoyable, all you have to do is let that energy come across and people will respond positively.

Now, don't go overboard. Don't make empty statements of praise or promises you can't back up. You want to be enthusiastic, but not foolhardy. In fact, it might be best to write out what you want to say, putting as much passion into it as you can, and then have someone else look at it. Even looking at it yourself the next day may show you where you need to tone things down a bit. But start big, and then edit yourself. Get that initial enthusiasm built into the piece, and then pull it back if necessary.

You do what you do for a reason beyond just the possibility of making money from it. What drew you to this field or industry in the first place? Why are you writing a blog on car repair or how people can do their own taxes? You may have spent hours, even years, developing your product or your knowledge and skills. So why did you do all that, and what makes your new invention so much better than anything else out there? You know what drives you. Now you just have to convince your prospects that they need to know what you know.

If you are writing ad or website copy for someone else, you will have to get your enthusiasm from learning more about the product or service from your client (or friend). Before you start, find out what makes it so great by getting the story from someone who knows. Then do what you can to convey that feeling into your writing.

LESSON 7: SHOWMANSHIP WILL DIFFERENTIATE YOU

Nobody is going to make the effort to read something that looks uninteresting. There's just too much to distract us these days. People's attention spans are getting more and more abbreviated. If you want to influence people's behavior, you have to grab and hold their interest long enough to get your message across. Sometimes that takes a little showmanship.

We talked in depth about tricks of showmanship back in Chapter 2. Look at that section again, and consider how you can apply some of those ideas for yourself. What can you do that will make your sales piece or banner ad or TV commercial or job application really stand out from everything else competing for your prospect's attention?

Physically, there are clearly things you can do. If you're sending out a direct mail package, you can use a brightly colored envelope. You can use attention-getting graphics, or place wording on the envelope that's a little intriguing or even a bit outrageous. You can send out some kind of lumpy mail—an envelope containing something that feels bulky and interesting. When prospects pick it up, they can tell there's something inside and their curiosity drives them to check it out.

If you're promoting yourself online, you can use intriguing headlines or images on banner ads or choose blog titles that will capture interest. You can also use blinking banner ads or video ads. And a bit of showmanship in the subject line of an email can lead to a better open rate.

If you want your job application to stand out from all the others a company receives, you can use an unusual envelope—maybe one with color or a string tie closure. You can send it by FedEx to make it look especially important or enclose samples of your work packaged in an interesting way.

A little showmanship can make the difference between being overlooked and being noticed. Unless it's noticed, your message will never get through. Don't go overboard, though, because there's a fine line between showmanship and clownishness, which could hurt your case. Make sure that anything you do as a form of showmanship is appropriate for the audience you're trying to reach. Don't use language or graphics to get attention that will be offensive to your target audience—that will get you the kind of attention you don't want!

LESSON 8: BE CLEAR AND CONSISTENT

Once you've worked so hard to capture your prospects' attention, you don't want to lose it too quickly. In the best of worlds, your prospects will stay with you until you've presented your entire pitch. Whether you're designing a website or putting together a direct mail piece, there are certain steps you can take that will make it easier for your prospects to hang in there long enough to get the message and respond to it. Here are some of the things you can do:

▪ *Simple language.* Don't try to impress people with your fancy vocabulary or long, convoluted sentences. People want to read quickly and get the message without having to struggle to figure out what you're saying. Use simple sentence structures, shorter sentences, and shorter paragraphs.

Having said that, write in a way that's appropriate for your audience. If your website is providing scientific information to doctors, you would obviously want to use the appropriate language, even though it would be too difficult for a lay audience. Even then, don't be more complicated than you need to be. Get your message across clearly and succinctly.

▪ *Easy-to-read visuals.* There's an art to designing copy visually so that people want to read it. Choose a font that is easy to read, and make it big enough for the average person to see. Make it a little bigger if your prospects are senior citizens.

Consider the use of color judiciously. Light-colored type on a white background may look nice from a design point of view, but it is impossible to read. People will take one look and not even try to read it. A shorter line length makes it easier for the eye to sweep back and forth without getting lost.

If you're designing for the web and mobile devices, you don't always have control over what people will see. Check out your design on a number of different devices to make sure it works on all of them.

▪ *Appealing design.* Which would you rather read: a solid block of gray type, or type broken up into paragraphs with headlines and subheads, pull quotes and sidebars, with pictures and graphics?

We all prefer to look at something that's interesting and attractive, and that doesn't look like reading it would give us eyestrain. A big part of any message is its presentation. Don't expect people to slog through your sales message just because you've put it out there. They won't. But make it appealing to look at, and they just might.

▌ *Clear call to action.* One of the biggest mistakes I see promoters make is such a simple one to avoid that it makes me want to call them up and ask them what they were thinking—or if they were thinking at all. They created an extensive and carefully crafted message. They design it to be beautiful, appealing, and easy to read. They do such a good job that they actually get people to read the whole thing. And then they drop the ball by failing to include a clear call to action. In other words, they don't tell their prospects what they are supposed to do next. If you don't tell people what to do, they won't do anything at all.

One of my favorite examples of this is a four-color postcard I received from a local hospital introducing two new surgeons they had just hired. The card was beautiful and expensive to print and mail, but it wasn't clear why they had sent it. There was no call to action. There was a phone number printed on the card, but it didn't say to call if you think you might need surgery, or for a free health screening, or for a second opinion. They should have gotten a second opinion on the postcard before they mailed it! Maybe they were hoping people would file the card away until the day they needed a surgeon. If that was the case, they should have at least suggested that.

Don't make their mistake. Make your offer clear, and tell people what they should do next. Without that, everything else you accomplish with your promotional materials is a waste.

▌ *Clear contact information and ordering instructions.* An essential part of a clear call to action is telling people exactly how they should respond. If you want them to click a link, make the link prominent and say "Click Here to Order." If you want them to call, make the phone number easy to find. Try to keep ordering instructions simple, but if the options are a little complex, spell them out as clearly as possible. Don't rely on your prospects to figure out on their own what you want them to do. Make it easy for them to do what you want.

LESSON 9: "ADVERTISING OPPORTUNITIES ARE NOW INFINITE"

Brian got the above quote from an investment banker he met in New York. And it really is true. There's more available media today than there ever has been in the history of marketing. And there will only be more in the future.

This was something the legends didn't know was coming, but everything they have taught us can be used in any medium—now and in the future. Let's quickly summarize some of the ways to reach people these days.

- *Online* through websites, blogs, social media, banner ads, email campaigns, sites like Craigslist, and so on
- *Ads in publications* like local newspapers, national newspapers, and magazines
- *Radio or TV* through spot ads, paid programming, shopping networks, and getting yourself interviewed
- *Direct mail*, where you send out sales pieces to lists of specially selected names

Your overall marketing plan will depend in part on your budget and resources, but also on selecting the medium that will best reach your target audience.

So we come back to the issue of knowing who your best prospects are. Do they read magazines? Do they watch television? Do they spend most of their time on social media? If your product is designed for teenagers, you will probably be wasting your time and money buying advertising in the local paper, unless you think their parents can convince them they need your product. Sometimes a multipronged approach works best. For example, you might use social media backed up by a direct mail campaign. But how will you know for sure what to do?

That brings us to our last point . . .

LESSON 10: TESTING TRUMPS ALL

Brian reminded me of one of the rules of thumb from direct mail great Dick Benson:

No mailer tests enough.

If there's one thing our legends all agreed on and emphasized in their writing and thinking, it was that testing is everything in marketing. Hopefully after reading this book, you will become someone who tests more than enough. Don't rest on your laurels by assuming you're getting the best results possible. And don't assume that something you're doing isn't working at all and should be dropped. One small change in a headline or color you use can turn a losing campaign into a winner.

You never have to grope around in the dark. You can use very simple methods for running statistical tests that will show you exactly where you stand with your promotional efforts, and how every change you make affects your results.

If you are not measuring your response rates, you could be missing out on better results or wasting your money altogether. Learn how to assess the results of your campaigns: it could make the difference between just getting by and having a smashing success. If you've never done any testing, and you'd like a brief introduction to the testing process, visit TheAdvertisingSolution.com and read my article "Tracking for Gold."

Once again, here is the list of The Top Ten Lessons from the Legends:

1. Know your product
2. Know your audience
3. Get started
4. Make sure you get every part of the package right
5. It's all about the prospect
6. Be passionate about what you're selling

7. Showmanship will differentiate you
8. Be clear and consistent
9. "Advertising opportunities are now infinite"
10. Testing trumps all

FINAL WORDS

Promoting yourself or a product is part art, part science. Not everyone can have the genius of one of these legends, but everyone can use these principles to create campaigns that get their message across and move people to action.

In this book, we've presented the findings and practices of some of the best minds in the business. And we looked at how you can apply what they did to whatever it is you are doing now. Don't hesitate to try new things. Experiment and learn as you go. Keep testing your results and you will find that your ability to influence others grows with every effort you make.

To help you continue your studies and develop your skills we've created a website, www.TheAdvertisingSolution.com. Visit any time to find valuable free resources and legendary swipe files.

ABOUT THE AUTHORS

CRAIG SIMPSON

Craig Simpson is the owner of Simpson Direct, Inc., based out of Grants Pass, Oregon. Since beginning his career in direct marketing nearly 20 years ago, he has managed thousands of marketing campaigns, helping to gross hundreds of millions of dollars in revenue for his clients.

His direct marketing company manages almost 300 different promotions per year. He works in practically every industry, marketing everything from auto and RV dealerships to technical software, retail stores, real estate investment, financial services, legal professionals, diet programs, insurance, and health and beauty products.

Craig's knowledge of direct marketing techniques has helped him become one of the nation's leading experts in direct marketing. He is regularly asked to speak at national events.

He is married and has three children. You can contact Craig at www.Simpson-Direct.com.

BRIAN KURTZ

Brian Kurtz has been a serial direct marketer for over 35 years and never met a medium he didn't like.

Under Brian's marketing leadership at direct marketing giant, Boardroom Inc., revenues grew from approximately $5 million (in 1981) to a high of almost $160 million in 2006.

Over his 34 years at Boardroom Inc., before leaving the company in February of 2015, he was responsible for the mailing of over 1.5 billion pieces of direct mail; the distribution of millions of impressions and promotions in all media including print, TV, and online, using state-of-the art techniques; built print and electronic newsletter businesses, reaching millions of subscribers; and he worked with the most successful copywriters and consultants in direct marketing, including Eugene Schwartz who is profiled in *The Advertising Solution*.

In addition to selling millions of subscriptions, Brian's efforts led to the sales of tens of millions of books directly to consumers, mostly in health and financial categories.

In September 2014, Brian hosted what has been called the event of the decade: "Titans of Direct Response."

"Titans" brought together the greatest minds in direct response marketing from the last 50 years . . . both as speakers and attendees. Information on the epic conference is at www.TitansOf DirectResponse.com.

Brian writes and speaks regularly—recent content can be found at www.briankurtz.me. He also runs two high end Mastermind Groups for marketers, entrepreneurs, and copywriters. And he consults and advises bleeding edge direct marketing companies and business leaders in a wide variety of areas.

However, Brian is really just a Little League Baseball Umpire with his eyes on the ultimate prize: A shot at umpiring in the Little League World Series. And he hopes it happens while he is still upright . . . and soon.

INDEX

TheAdvertisingSolution.com
Where the Eternal Truths of Marketing Live Forever

Dear Future Legend,

The six advertising legends profiled in this book are heroes of ours, and we hope they are now heroes of yours too.

We want to continue sharing what we learned putting together this book, and also share what we learn about many more legends in the months and years to come.

Please visit **www.TheAdvertisingSolution.com** to find out even more about:

- Techniques for getting your message noticed and remembered
- What you can learn from the best headlines of all time
- How to track the success of your campaigns so they get better and better each time you run one
- How to prepare yourself to handle the flood of responses your campaigns bring in

You will also find:

- Access to hard-to-find swipe files from past and current legends
- Feedback and insight from experts on many of the concepts covered in *The Advertising Solution*
- And anything else we can find that would be helpful for your marketing efforts

TheAdvertisingSolution.com is your powerful FREE resource committed to helping you grow your business.

To your continued success,
Craig and Brian